Financial Planning Exposed:
Overcoming Myths to Create a
Secure Future

MARGIE SHARD, CFP®

Cover Illustration Copyright © 2014 by Margie Shard
Cover design by Shard Marketing and Branding
Chapter illustrations and infographics © 2014 Margie Shard
Author photograph by Emma Burcusel Photography
Editing by Kate-Madonna Hindes

ISBN: 0692354190
ISBN-13: 978-0692354193

DEDICATION

This book is dedicated to all the clients I've had the privilege of working with over the years. Thank you for teaching me just as much as I've taught you.

To my team at Shard Financial Services, Amanda McCall and Jen Verscheure, thank you for always putting our clients first, going above and beyond, and having the desire to learn more. To Yussef Gheriani, thank you for stepping in and quickly doing final grammatical edits.

To Antonio Ayala, thank you for being creative and working with me on numerous revisions. I know that you had many late nights working on this project and I really appreciate your positive attitude and the fact that you never complain.

To my husband Tony Shard, thank you for always putting our family first, jumping in to help me without any second thoughts, and being my number one fan. I love you more than I could ever express.

To my brilliant son Keegan, you inspire me every day. I love your smile and laughter and how it brightens my life. I'm so proud of the little boy you are today, and the man that you will become someday, although way too soon. I love you and thank you for the joy you bring to my life.

CONTENTS

FOREWORD

No financial planning book out there is addressing the lack of thoughtful and individualistic-based service lacking in my industry. If you turn on any television program or listen to any radio station, they address investments and financial planning as a whole unit. However, most of my clients have very unique scenarios and need individualized planning services. These plans coordinate goals and lifestyles along with investment strategies.

In this book, I discuss many of the myths perpetrated by those in my industry. Each chapter will break down myths, one-by-one, and give real-world advice as well as recommendations if you find yourself in a similar scenario.

I'm not here to simply help you with money; I'm here to create a pathway for you to achieve your goals. Ask yourself these 10 questions before you get started:

1. What do you want to financially accomplish in the next year? 5 years? 10 years?
2. Do you have a coordinated plan for your investment that is tax-efficient?
3. Do you know if you are on track to meet your retirement goals?
4. If your spouse/partner died or became disabled, would you be able to survive?
5. If you had to go buy a car or rent housing, would you be able to do it without a co-signor?
6. Do you have money left each month or does your debt just grow?
7. Are you responsibly managing your credit? Do you know what is on your credit report?

8. Do you feel overwhelmed and don't know where to start?

9. Do you fully understand your retirement plan options through your employer and are you taking advantage of the benefits?

10. Do you have too much cash sitting in the bank not earning anything because you don't know what to do with it? Do you have a cash surplus plan?

This book is about questioning the long-held myths of the retirement industry and what you can do to be an educated and thoughtful consumer. My hope is that as you read this book, you will stop and think about the impact your financial situation has on not only yourself, but also the rest of your family. If I can stress any point to you, it's that every individual, whether they have a single dollar or millions of dollars in the bank, should see a financial planner to know what their future financial path holds. Your future success rests on the choices you are making now.

You deserve to live the best retirement ever, on your terms.

James and Sarah's Retirement Story:

I recently had new clients, James and Sarah, come into my office believing they didn't need financial planning. I started asking them about their family, what their goals were, and how much they had saved. Sarah told me that they had three children, 14, 13, and 11. They planned on paying for their college in full, and thought that it shouldn't be that much because they were going to attend in-state schools. She also explained that they were looking to upgrade their home in the next year and that they wanted to retire in 15 years.

"I just don't really believe in all of this stuff," James replied. His wife Sarah looked at me and said, "Well, I do and I think we need a plan."

When I asked what they had saved towards college James told me that they didn't need to save anything since they were going to just "cash flow it." I quickly did a calculation in my head and asked if they had between $25,000 and $100,000 of excess cash after they paid their taxes and bills each year.

James started laughing. "Of course I don't have that much! I have three kids. If we have anything left at the end of the month we are lucky!"

"How are you going to pay for their college?" I asked.
James had no idea why I was asking this simple question.

"Well, if you are going to utilize your cash flow, remember that annual tuition, books, and room and boarding fees at in-state schools are approximately $25,000 in today's dollars. College costs increase by about 5% per year, and at one point you will have all three kids in college at once."

Sarah gave me a scared look. James became very quiet. "That's a lot of money." He said.

"Yes it is. Let me ask you about your house. How much equity are you rolling into your next house?"

"We don't have equity. We will barely get out of it without having to pay something. The new mortgage costs we are looking at are only an additional $400 per month." Sarah told me.

"What have you saved for retirement?" I asked them.

"I have $150,000 in my 401(k) at work and an IRA with $33,000. Sarah has $255,000 in a Simple IRA and she also has a Roth IRA with $6,500 in it," James said.

"Ok, so let's approximate that you have $450,000. What do you believe you can receive in income on your approximate $450,000?" I asked.

"I'm guessing $50,000 a year." James said.

"That would be 11% + per year. That's more than double what you should be able to potentially pull without taking the chance of outliving your income."

"Do you have any pensions?"

"No."

"Ok. Well in the last five minutes you just told me you don't need financial planning, but, you are planning to cash flow your three kids' college funds and add an additional $400 to your monthly mortgage payment even though as you put 'if we have anything left at the end of the month we are lucky.' You want to retire in 15 years and should only take about half of what you expect to pull. By the time your last child graduates, if she does it in four years, then you will be only four years away from retirement. Does this sound correct?"

Both Sarah and James nodded hesitantly.

"Do you still think you don't need planning?" I asked.

Sarah and James looked at each other and then back at me. "Ok, you made your point. What do we need to do?" James asked.

The reason I tell you this story is not to belittle Sarah and James. I tell you this story because their story is very typical. Most people do not understand what financial planning is. Furthermore, those who work with a financial/investment advisor think that means they have done financial planning. Most people do not have a true financial plan, they have unrealistic expectations about what they can and should do with their money. This leads to bad financial decision making and retirements that are not the retirement life people envisioned.

Chapter 1
FINANCIAL PLANNING EXPOSED:
FINANCIAL PLANNERS VS. FINANCIAL ADVISORS

Myth #1: A Financial Advisor (or investment advisor) is the same as a Financial Planner.

Myth #2: General financial advice can be applied to everyone's situation, so a detailed plan that is customized isn't necessary.

Myth #3: A hypothetical calculation of what the future value of your account could grow to is a financial plan.

Myth #1: A Financial Advisor (or Investment Advisor) is the same as a Financial Planner.

Imagine this. You fall down the stairs and believe you may have broken your arm. Instead of going to the hospital, you go see your family doctor. The doctor asks you what is wrong and you explain you believe it's a broken arm. The doctor touches your arm in a few spots and immediately says, "Yes! You did break your arm!" He then looks at you and says, "Before we put it in a cast we need to perform a surgery and break it in several more places so it will heal correctly."

"Shouldn't I get an X-ray?"

"No, that isn't necessary," the doctor replies.

"Shouldn't I have a surgeon look at my arm?"

"No. I can do it," says the doctor.

The doctor then orders his nurse to give you anesthesia in order to perform surgery on your arm.

"Hold on! I want an X-ray!"

Sounds unbelievable right? Instead of you breaking your arm, imagine you are breaking your financial future. Retirement planning is important and needs the right professional.

The problem is this happens all the time. I constantly see new clients come in who are told by their financial advisor they are all set for retirement; who have unrealistic expectations about their money because their financial advisor isn't doing financial planning, but is instead telling them everything is fine.

What I have found is the general public believes they have a financial planner, when in truth they only have a financial advisor. There is a big difference. It isn't the general public's fault either. There isn't much education surrounding this topic.

Herein lies the tragedy: We are in a time where people need financial planning more than ever. Life expectancy is longer, medical bills are higher, social security is in a dire state, and consumer debt is out of control. We are in a time where interest rates are still low, but will start to climb. This causes a chain reaction in bond prices declining. People generally throw their "safe money" into bonds and it will no longer be so safe there. The stock market just went through one of the worst bear markets to-date and not everyone has recovered. Pensions are getting rarer and those who still have pensions are now getting buy-out options. Some people lost their pensions due to failure of companies and mismanagement. Individuals are scared to invest in their retirement plans through work because they don't understand them. Really, you get the point, right?

People need planning, more than ever. Yet, most people who work with a financial advisor are not getting planning, but believe they are. They are given unrealistic expectations by their advisors because the advisors are not looking at the entire picture. Mistakes are being made and opportunities are being lost. However, this can be stopped.

It's time for the general public to really understand what kind of financial professional they are working with, what they need to be discussing and expecting when planning for retirement.

So what is the big difference between financial advisors and financial planners?

Financial advisors don't look in depth at your entire financial situation. They may ask general questions, but they are not getting into the unique details of your financial life and lifestyle. Financial advisors typically only manage investments and will give a general overview of your situation. They may run a few hypothetical situations about what your future value may be or what you need to save each month/year in order to get to a certain value, but it isn't truly personalized. This is a huge detriment to your future, one you need to know about. You deserve personalized advice, suited to your situation, not advice coming from a big book or old methodologies.

Financial planners dig deep into your financial life. They are looking at your cash flow: your incomes, expenses, tax returns, surpluses or deficits. They look at your net worth: your liquid assets both on the retirement and non-retirement sides. This includes your non-liquid assets like real estate and the cash flows. Most importantly, financial planners look into your debts and all the important information like interest rates, repayment schedules, and tax benefits you may or may not have.

Financial planners talk in-depth about your goals and lifestyle. They discuss the expenses you have and how they may change in your retirement, especially if a spouse or partner passes away. Financial planners ask you about your needs and wants. These professionals also create different scenarios and incorporate inflation and rates of return, as well as your life expectancy. Pension, social security, and other income source scenarios are created and discussed to look at your life from a 360-degree angle. They review your plan periodically and make sure your investments still fit your current and long term needs. Can you see the difference?

By running your plan and looking at your specific needs and wants, financial planners are able to best incorporate your investments to meet your plan goals. They can design investment strategies incorporating tax-efficiencies for traditional investments like stocks and bonds, as well as alternative investments that can help you meet your goals. It is a full, comprehensive approach and it involves more than just one meeting. It also involves both the financial planner and the client having open, honest discussions that may not always involve fun topics. However, these discussions are typically some of the most important discussions you can have to lead to a happy retirement and protection for you and your family.

Here are a few of the documents your financial planner should be reviewing: (Discuss with your Financial Planner what else you should be bringing to your appointment.)

- Statements of investment accounts
- Taxes
- Social Security Statements
- Pension Information
- Paycheck Stubs
- Estate Planning Documents
- Insurance Policies

Hear It From An Expert: If you're meeting with a financial planner for the first time after you retire, you may or may not be able to change your situation. Seek a financial planner out well before retirement to ensure they can put you on track to meet your goals and save the amount of money you need. Clients outliving their retirement savings is one of the most preventable mistakes I see. By adjusting expectations and planning correctly in the beginning, continuing to monitor progress, and implement necessary changes, my clients have a much higher chance of avoiding this tragic scenario.

	Advisors	Planners
Investment Management	✓	✓
Run Hypothetical Rates of Return	✓	✓
College Calcluations for Amounts to Save	✓	✓
Review Expenses and Cash Flow	X	✓
Create Debt Elimination/Management Plan	X	✓
Inflate Expenses for Retirement Assumptions	X	✓
Create Income/Distribution Solutions	X	✓
Create Tax Efficient Investment Scenarios	X	✓
Pension Income/Buyout/Rollover Calculations	X	✓
Social Security Strategy Calculations	X	✓
In-Depth Risk Analysis to Determine Insurance Amounts	X	✓

Myth #2: General financial advice can be applied to everyone's situation, so a detailed and customized plan is not necessary.

Financial advice and parenting advice are very similar. Anyone who has had unsolicited information understands: Sometimes, the advice-giver doesn't recognize all the important details of a certain situation and the advice doesn't apply. My mother often told me she had three children and each one of them was different from the others. Parenting is difficult because parents need to relate on an individual basis to each one of their children.

I didn't understand what my mother really meant until just recently. My son was diagnosed with a medical condition that took me by surprise. I needed a team who could answer my questions in a way I could understand and then make a decision on behalf of my family. I accepted a professional's advice at face value and later came to regret it.

Ultimately, I had to trust my gut about who those people were and what route of treatment to take with my child. And I've learned through my own personal story that my child learns differently and is very brilliant, but general parenting advice just does not work. I needed to build a team that understood all the details of my life, including my values and beliefs. To better help my son, I needed to listen to my gut and readjust my expectations.

Having to educate myself so I could be my son's best advocate was intimidating, frustrating, and time consuming. However, that process was time well spent because it allowed me to choose the right team to help me recover my child. The same process has helped me shape my financial planning practice.

> **As each child is different, so is each person's financial plan. It's important to recognize your future goals are dependent on advice and planning you choose today. Build a team that can help you correctly assess your needs and prepare for a successful future.**

I believe in exactly what I tell my clients: research your options and build a financial team you can trust, so they can guide you, educate you, and help you make the best decisions for you and your family.

Your financial future is not the same as the futures of others around you. Unsolicited advice or advice given through blanket statements can actually harm your future retirement dreams.

Hear It From An Expert: Your financial situation is unique. Listening to generalized advice and not understanding if it even applies to your current situation is detrimental. A financial planner who takes into consideration all the aspects of your life should be making recommendations based on your best interests. Many solutions may exist and it's a financial planner's job to design a financial strategy best suited to get you to your goals.

A Note on Celebrity "Experts"

You've heard all about them: They have books, radio programs and TV shows. The "industry experts" or celebrity financial advisors dispense advice to the public with zest, but without a lot of details. The reason I put "experts" in quotations is because most of these people don't even have the proper qualifications. To truly give the best advice, I feel a financial planner needs a financial planning certificate, issued by the CERTIFIED FINANCIAL PLANNER™ Board. Financial advisors should have insurance certification, Series 7- (securities registration) and a Series 65 or 66, (for managed money.) If your advisor only has a Series 6 then they can only sell you prospectus products. If they don't have a 65 or 66 then the advisor can only invest your money on a commission basis vs an actively managed, fee based, advisory account . Having an advisor with the proper licenses so different investments can be taken into consideration for your individual situation is important.

Celebrity Experts are in a business and their business is to give the most generalized advice possible, sell as many programs, licenses, etc., and to generate revenue. Remember that!

I am not saying there isn't any good advice given by these celebrity "experts." However, as with any media driven business, they get paid by promoting their program. They can't give individualized advice because without all the details and proper credentials, these experts could face a lawsuit.

Pension and Spending Story:
I had met with a couple once who really needed a guaranteed stream of income. They were not able to control their spending habits and were in debt. Basically, the couple was making poor choices, had no savings, and had lost their house in foreclosure.

They came to me because they had to make a pension decision. Either they could take a $750,000 lump sum or they could stay with the pension company and get a lifetime payout.

What they needed was a guaranteed income for the rest of their lives. They had gone to a workshop at their church. They had started listening to the celebrity expert's radio show as well. This actually should have been a positive step, but they failed to make the changes necessary to get out of debt and stop creating more.

They told me they believed wholeheartedly in what this celebrity said, but after six months all they had done was get into more debt. They could not control their spending. After meeting with them I recommended that they roll their money over only if they were going to go into an annuity with a guaranteed stream of income, which would give both spouses a higher lifetime payout than what they could receive if they left it at the current pension company. I also told them that if they rolled their money and had access to it that it was my belief they would spend it in under 5 years and would be left with only their social security checks.

Because they listened to this radio celebrity (who had no investment credentials), they decided an annuity was a bad investment. They couldn't tell me why it was bad, only that, "He said not to invest in an annuity".

They said they wanted to roll their money to an IRA with no guaranteed stream of income. I gave them some examples of people who had won the lotto and spent their millions of dollars of winnings in only a few years. Due to their spending habits, I told them I believed they too, would end up spending their money and I wouldn't advise rolling their money. I refused to bring them on as a client.

They ended up rolling their money to an IRA with another advisor. One of my clients, who had originally referred them to me, told me they spent the entire amount within 3 years and were now living with their children.

I had another client who was an avid fan of a financial "celebrity expert" on TV. My client would watch this person's show faithfully and was always quoting what the "celebrity expert" said.

Celebrity Expert Story:
One day my client called me in a panic. "I was watching her show today and she said, "If you don't understand the stock market, you

should just go into bonds." We need to sell all of my stocks and go into bonds because I don't really understand how the market works."

I explained to my client she was in a well-diversified portfolio currently meeting her financial objectives and I would be happy to give her some more education on how the stock market works.

I further explained that her portfolio was paying higher dividends than the current interest rates on bonds. We would not be able to match the income she was getting in bonds since interest rates had fallen so low. Once rates went back up, the price on the bonds would fall. I told my client if we sold her stocks, the tax consequences were also going to be disastrous for her as it would generate hefty capital gains. During this meeting my client kept saying to me, "But she said to get out of the stock market and go into bonds if I don't fully understand the stock market…"

I kept explaining to her that her "celebrity expert" gives generalized investment advice and it doesn't apply to everyone. What was said on TV was irrelevant to my client's situation, yet my client idolized this "celebrity expert" and thought everything they said had worth.

My client wouldn't agree to keep her stocks. I asked her to move her account to another firm because I was not going to be responsible for the disaster about to take place.

She moved her account to another local firm and I saw her about eight months later. She came into my office and told me that she had a $45,000 tax bill, had to reduce her income because the bonds weren't paying anything near the income the stocks had paid, had paid her new financial advisor over $15,000 in commission on the purchase of her new bonds, and her bond prices had also dropped.

"I'm afraid I am going to run out of my money now," she told me. "What do I do now and will you help me?"

"You need to reduce your expenses and take a smaller income off of your accounts or you will run out of money," I explained to her.

"I don't want to reduce my expenses," she said.

"Unfortunately, those are your two choices. You have done damage that can not be fixed overnight and now you need to stop the bleeding." I told her.

She did ultimately decide to reduce her expenses. Her standard of living has still not recovered from the decisions she made listening to her favorite "celebrity expert's" poor advice.

The bottom line is this: Your financial planner should sit with you, be able to look you in the eyes, and listen to your unique situation. You need to build your financial team of professionals who can help guide you along the way based on what you need for your financial life. If you're inclined to listen to someone online, or on the radio, bring their points to your financial planner to discuss.

Myth #3: A hypothetical calculation of what the future value of your account could grow to is a financial plan.

Often new clients will come in and say, "My financial advisor, they told me I'm all set for retirement," when in fact, they are nowhere near it.

Or a new client who is already retired will come in and say, "My financial advisor told me that I was all set for retirement, but I'm running out of my money."

When I ask if they had a financial plan done before they retired, they will tell me yes and pull out a hypothetical illustration showing the value of their accounts with a hypothetical growth and distribution rate. The illustration is just that - a hypothetical illustration. It doesn't account for taxes, expenses, inflation or lifestyle goals. It also doesn't account for perceived risks.

Vince's Retirement Story:
Vince was referred to me after his wife died. She had died on the job and after three and a half years, the insurance company had finally settled. He had received a $750,000 settlement and had another $150,000 in retirement assets. Vince was 58 and no longer working having been laid off from his previous employer. He had no other sources of income until he turned 60 and would be eligible to pull a Social Security widows benefit of $1,200 per month.

Vince's attorney encouraged him to come see me because the financial advisor who had been managing the $150,000 retirement account told him he was all set for retirement. The referring attorney was concerned about Vince because he had discussed several expensive things he was planning to do with his settlement.

Vince wanted to put a $75,000 addition on his house. He also was looking to buy a $250,000 home in another state. Vince's attorney encouraged him to come see me, so I could run a full financial plan on him.

When I met with Vince he showed me the hypothetical illustration that his advisor had ran for him. It assumed a 10% annual return and had Vince pulling 7% a year ($63,000) of his total portfolio value.

There was also another page that had Vince's basic necessity expenses - food, shelter, etc. - but had no luxury expenses such as vacations, hobbies, donations, etc. I started asking Vince about his expenses and the reality was Vince's expenses exceeded the 7% ($63,000) the advisor had illustrated. The true expenses based on his current lifestyle were $85,000 per year.

I asked Vince what his advisor had said when he told him he was planning on taking the two lump sums totaling $300,000 out of his account.
Vince stated, "He told me that we would just have to pull a little more out than we wanted, but that we could go more aggressive in the next few years to make up for it."

I had a discussion with Vince about how the market works and how an aggressive investment strategy in retirement wasn't a smart thing to do. We also discussed how a 7% withdrawal rate was much higher than the 4-5% recommended rate once retired. Furthermore, if Vince did pull the $300,000 out of his account he would have to actually withdraw over 14% out in order to get the $85,000 needed to maintain his current standard of living. At that rate, he was at a great risk of spending down his accounts in the next 10-15 years.

I met with Vince a few more times and we discussed different choices he could make instead of the addition and vacation home. Vince ended up renting a house down south for four months during the winter instead of buying. He also decided all he really wanted was a sunroom on his primary residence so it cut the expenses down from $75,000 to $20,000.

Vince also had debt, so we agreed on a debt elimination plan reducing his expenses $13,000 per year.

Vince has withdrawn money out of his account for over six years, but because we put a strong financial plan in place, he was able to make better financial choices and the value of his account has grown. When I met with Vince this past year, I told him if he needed a raise in his income we could increase his withdrawal rate, but he told me that he was living how he wanted too and didn't need it right now. "I'm just grateful I came to you when I did because before I met you I thought I was all set to do what I originally planned with my money since I had almost a million dollars."

Vince's retirement continues to look bright. Because he took the time to do financial planning, he was able to avoid making huge financial mistakes that would have cost him his retirement.

Your retirement is too important to just make assumptions. Your financial advisor is probably not accounting for inflation, taxes, and future dreams. Your portfolio and financial plan will change with your life choices. If you have a million dollars, don't assume you can retire. Your individual lifestyle, habits, goals, and hobbies will determine if it's enough or not. Make sure you have realistic expectations for what your money can really do for you.

Hear It From An Expert: Financial planning before you start to take distributions is important. If you want to prevent running out of your money, do your homework! Sometimes compromises in what you want need to be made in order to not outlive your income. Just because you are close to or have a million dollars does not necessarily mean you are able to retire. Find an actual financial planner and consult them before major financial decisions are made. You will be happy you did.

Resources

www.letsmakeaplan.org
www.consumerfinance.gov

Chapter 2
FINANCIAL PLANNING EXPOSED:
DEBT, TAXES, AND OUTLIVING YOUR RETIREMENT

Myth #1: As long as your payments on your debt are low and manageable, debt really is not a big deal.

Myth #2: The amount of annual income you need day one of retirement will be the same throughout your retirement.

Myth #3: Retirees do not pay a lot in taxes, or, the tax burden is significantly smaller.

Myth #1: As long as your payments on your debt are low and manageable, debt really is not a big deal.

Debt is something that can really harm your retirement. When I start discussing debt with my clients, it's an eye opener for them to see how debt in retirement can really spend down their assets. The sooner in life you pay off your debt and redirect your excess cash to investments, the more financially secure your retirement should be. If you are 5 years out, it is crucial you take a hard look at your debt and get on a debt elimination plan.

Lisa's Debt Story:

I recently had a new client Lisa referred to me by an attorney. She is in her 60's and is looking to retire in the next three to five years. She was specifically looking for a Certified Financial Planner and came to me because her current financial advisor had told her she was all set for retirement but Lisa felt like something wasn't right.

When Lisa first came to me we discussed her current situation. She was recently divorced and didn't receive a lot of the assets that her prior ex-husband was awarded.

She was looking to retire in three to five years but also worked at a company that might have been moving out of state, possibly forcing her to retire sooner than expected. She had been awarded the marital house in the divorce which cost her $36,000 per year between mortgage payments, taxes, insurance, and upkeep.

During our first meeting when I asked about the house I could tell I had hit a nerve. Lisa was adamant she would not move. She had raised her children in the house and was not going to let go of those memories.

I didn't even have to run a full plan to know Lisa was not going to be able to retire in three to five years without the risk of outliving her money. Still, I ran the plan.

Change is hard and many times telling a client what they need to do is a difficult conversation because it involves emotions and sacrifice in order to make things better. If a client isn't willing to change, then I can't help them. I knew before going into my meeting with Lisa it was going to be a difficult conversation and I really didn't know which way it was going to go.

I presented the plan to Lisa. I showed her how she was at risk of running out of her money within 8 years of retirement. I explained to her we had to reduce her expenses if she was going to have a fighting chance.

"I know that you expressed to me that you don't want to move, but you really cannot afford that house. The housing market has picked up a little and the approximate $150,000 of equity you have in your house could be used to buy a new house outright. It would reduce your expenses by approximately $24,000 a year."

"I just think that there has to be another way," Lisa said.

I moved the discussion forward as I could see it wasn't going to progress. I asked Lisa if she was surprised the effect inflation had on her savings.

Lisa told me how her old advisor hadn't looked at her expenses, taken inflation into consideration, or really looked at all of her goals. "I just felt like something wasn't right."

When Lisa left my office that day, she looked me in the eye and told me she was going to think about her housing situation.

Fast forward to three months later, Lisa came into my office for a review. A glowing smile revealed that Lisa had been working fast and furious on her pre-retirement homework. She had put her house on the market and had a buyer, had reduced a number of other expenses, started contributing again to her 401(k) plan at work, and was thinking of further ways to save money.

Lisa had also bought a new house that was only $100,000, so she got to keep another $56,000 from the sale of her old house.

Lisa was motivated and there was an excitement in the air. There was also a relief. Lisa is well on her way to a happy retirement. Due to her changes she went from running out of her money eight years after retiring to running out of her money 25 years after retiring.

When I asked Lisa what made her decide to leave the marital house behind, she told me, "I decided that my life was a lot more important than a house. I love that house, but I don't want my kids to have to support me someday because I put more value into that house than my own financial success."

While Lisa still isn't 100% where we both want her to be, she is much further towards meeting her goals than before. This really is an example of how important it is to start looking at your retirement situation before you retire and how looking at all the details are necessary – not just an estimate. Remember, it's your life and your retirement. You deserve to have all the facts so you can make the right decisions that will make you and your family happy and secure.

Here are the top three mistakes I see with debt:

1. Taking a mortgage or home equity loan out and investing the proceeds because rates are low

It still shocks me to see there are financial advisors who will tell their clients to take out a mortgage or home equity loan so they can use the proceeds to invest. This is not a smart thing to do. Your home and your liquid assets should not be commingled. It does not matter how low interest rates are. Do not put your house in the stock market or any other investment.

2. Taking loans against your 401(k) simply to, "borrow from yourself"

This is one of the biggest misconceptions out there. When you borrow from your 401(k), you have to pay an interest rate. Money you are contributing is now going to pay back debt and interest. You also create a double taxation situation because the loan repayment comes from your net, after-tax money. When you eventually take a distribution in retirement, you will have to pay taxes again on that money. If you leave your job before the loan is paid off, you typically only have 60 days to pay any remaining amount due or you will be taxed on the remaining balance. Furthermore, if you are under 59 ½ you will have to pay a 10% penalty as well.

3. Moving debt from one credit card to the other to save on interest rates

While interest rate swaps can make sense, constantly switching your balances from one card to another can just make your debt go up. Most cards have balance transfer fees of anywhere from 1-5% of the balance, along with a minimum amount. Make sure if you are going to transfer balances, that the balance transfer fee gets added into the equation to see if you are really coming out ahead.

Hear It From An Expert: When you look at having to create your income in retirement, and the fact that you have to still pay taxes on that income, it's easy to see why having to come up with monthly debt payments and then pay taxes on it is not ideal. Looking at your debt before you retire is critical. Utilizing your income while you are still working to pay off debt can pay off big down the road.

Brendon and Theresa's Retirement Story:
Brendon and Theresa were looking to retire in two years. Brendon worked for the government and had a pension. He had worked for 28 years and was going to be eligible to take an early retirement when he turned 58. Theresa had been a stay at home mom and worked part time on and off once they started their family.

When we first went through Brendon and Theresa's financial information, they had 3 credit cards that totaled $18,000. They also had a car loan that had another year of payments, and a mortgage of $53,000. They were paying minimums on everything.

They had savings of $10,000 for emergencies and Brendon had saved $550,000 in his 457 employer retirement plan. They also had been making contributions to IRA's and they each had $120,000 in account values.

They had previously been working with a financial advisor at their bank who managed their IRA's. The advisor had told them that they had enough saved for retirement and should be fine taking the early retirement in two years. Brendon and Theresa had come to see me because their friend Sam who previously had also worked with the same financial advisor had just gone through my financial planning process. Sam had explained to Brendon and Theresa that it was a lot more detailed than what the financial advisor had done and there were many risks and issues that needed to be addressed before he retired. Brendon and Theresa were curious as to what may have been missed.

When I asked them how the advisor concluded they were ok to retire in two years they told me they had supplied their living expenses and pension income. They showed me the information the advisor had requested and the projected income that the advisor had presented.

The expense sheet had their basic expenses such as housing, utilities, food, etc. It also included their minimum debt repayment needs. It had no luxury expenses such as vacations, gifts, hobbies, etc. I started asking Brendon and Theresa if they planned on traveling once they retired.

"Yes! We want to take an Alaskan cruise upon retirement. We currently take one vacation a year but once we retire we will probably take three to four vacations a year!" Theresa said. I then asked if they had any hobbies.

"I hunt. I go up north during deer season with my buddies for two weeks and I have always had a goal to hunt in Africa before I got too old." Brendon said.

"How much will your trip to Africa cost? $30,000? $40,000?" I asked.

"Probably $30,000."

The conversation continued. More expenses were revealed with even more costs that were not accounted for by their financial advisor. When we were done, the real expenses for Brendon and Theresa weren't the $45,000 per year their financial advisor had calculated. Their current expenses were $60,000 and their estimated retirement expenses were $85,000. That's a huge discrepancy!

We then started talking about inflation and how it would affect their portfolio. "As the cost of food, clothing, etc. increases, we will either need to reduce your standard of living and cut some of your luxury items, or we will need to pull more income off your investments. I see that your advisor has you taking the same amount of income each year. Does this mean you want to reduce your standard of living by perhaps cutting out your vacations or hobbies?"

Brendon and Theresa looked at each other in shock. "No, we don't want to reduce our standard of living and cut stuff out."

We then discussed their debt. "You currently are paying the minimum on all of your debt. Your mortgage is set to be paid off in 18 years. Your credit cards are set to be paid off in 33 years and your car will be paid off in a year. Does this sound correct?"

Brendon said, "Well when you put it like that it doesn't sound too good but yes, you are correct. Our financial advisor said that rates are low, so we don't really need to worry about it because my pension income can handle the payments. I can see that we have an entirely different situation than what our advisor has been looking at."

I explained to them the extra $9,500 they were spending per year on their house and credit cards was going to cost more because we had to pull it out of their retirement accounts and pay taxes on it.

By the time we got finished with creating a real financial plan for Brendon and Theresa, they realized that in order to have the retirement they wanted it made sense for Brendon to work till he was 60 instead of taking the early retirement at 58.

The two extra years of working actually gave Brendon and Theresa four years to add more to their retirement accounts and cut back on some expenses so they could focus on eliminating their debt. When we ran their financial plan, the difference of having to pay debt payments in retirement versus not having those debt payments was the difference of them running out of their money in 15 years versus 33 years.

We also looked at several scenarios to see what they realistically could spend on their luxury items during retirement. Instead of four big vacations a year, Brendon and Theresa set a budget of $10,000 per year to be utilized how they saw fit. We also inflated this number so they could keep up with the cost of living.

Brendon and Theresa have now been retired for a year. We just had the annual review of their plan and they told me how happy they were they spent the four prior years working on eliminating their debt. Furthermore, because their investments have done better than projected over the last few years, we actually increased their vacation budget to $15,000 per year. They just booked their Alaskan cruise and are happily retired.

Hear It From An Expert: I'm currently running financial plans for some of my clients with hypothetical rate of return on their current investment assets of 6% and an inflation rate of 3.72%, subject to change per client's goals and based on market and interest rate conditions. If your financial planner is not factoring taxes and inflation, they are not doing your planning justice.

Myth #2: The amount of annual income you need day one of retirement will be the same throughout your retirement.

In 1964, milk cost $0.93. Today it averages $3.93. Subway rides in Manhattan were only $0.15. Today it would cost $2.50. Minimum wage was $1.15 and now it was just raised to $10.00 in most states. The average price to go see a movie was $1.86. Today the average price is $29.

The overall message I'm trying to send is that inflation will happen. Costs will go up. It will get more expensive to live. Just because you are retired does not mean you will be able to avoid price increases. Not planning for price increases puts you at a high risk for outliving your income.

With life longevity on the rise, we need to plan for our savings to last 30, 40 and even 50+ years. Thinking we can retire and receive the same amount of income for the rest of our lives is not realistic.

Phil and Sally's Retirement Story:

Phil and Sally plan on working five more years before they retire. Here's what their debt looks like:

$83,000 mortgage balance which costs $18,000 per year

$22,000 unsecured debt which costs $3,120 per year paying the minimum balance

$5,000 car loan balance which costs $3,600 per year

If we look at Phil and Sally's expenses, they currently have a surplus of $7,000 per year which is usually used towards a vacation. They also have other luxury expenses of $35,000 per year, which include eating out, clothing, gifts, and more. Not including investment accounts, they have an additional $88,000 of cash sitting in a bank savings account, earning 0.5%.

Looking at their financial plan, Phil and Sally will need to come up with an additional $24,720 of after tax income in retirement to continue to pay the minimums on their debt. In their current tax bracket, they will need to pull an additional $8,240 per year for taxes. A total $32,960 will need to be pulled out of their retirement accounts. Pulling $32,960 extra from their retirement accounts will result in their accounts depleting prematurely. They will have a funding deficit of 23.6 years. In other words, they will run out of their money 23.6 years before their life expectancy.

On the other hand, if Phil and Sally have no debt, they should be able to live with their money and fund their retirement goals. If we review their luxury expenses of $35,000 and the $7,000 they typically spend on their vacation with their surplus cash, there is a $42,000 after tax amount of money to work with before they retire. If Phil and Sally can make some tough choices, they can start adding to debt payments and pay it off before retirement.

The total amount of debt owed is $110,000. After a discussion with Phil and Sally it is decided that they will take money out of their savings and pay off their car. They then can utilize the monthly payment to pay off their credit card debt.

They also decide they can reduce their vacation from $7,000 per year to $3,500. When looking at the rest of their luxury expenses, they cut out another $22,000 and redirect that to their debt. By doing this, Phil and Sally will have 100% of their debt paid off by the time they retire. They also will not be adding to their credit cards, a great habit to obtain before you retire. Having to change your lifestyle upon retirement is much harder than before you retire. Learning to live within a budget before you get on a fixed income is a good practice to have.

A note about outliving your retirement funds

Having helped clients since 2001, one of the biggest reasons I have seen individuals outlive their money is a major lack of planning before they retire. I often receive phone calls from individuals who want to meet with me after they retire. While some of these retirees are living a good life and are simply unhappy with their current investment professional, often I find myself sitting across my desk from retirees who are at a high risk of running out of money. Some of these retirees will have to completely downgrade their lifestyle in order to survive.

With life longevity on the rise, we need to plan for our savings to last 30, 40 and even 50+ years. Earlier this year CNBC, MSN, and other consumer media outlets starting addressing the Million Dollar Question. Analysts asked, "Do you really need a million dollars to retire?" In my career, I've found the answer is both yes and no. Consumers are often surprised to hear that for many, one million dollars will not be enough.

When discussing the longevity of retirement with clients, I often hear, "I won't live that long". However, according to the American Academy of Actuaries' public policy discussion paper "Risky Business: Living Longer without Income for Life" the average 65 year old couple has a 50/50 chance that one of them will live to be 90. To add to those statistics, the number of centenarians (those who live to be 100 years old and above,) are rapidly growing.

In 2009, The Associated Press published an article titled "Centenarians are the fastest-growing age segment: Number of 100-year-olds to hit 6 million by 2050". In this article they sited that in the 1950's there were only a few thousand estimated people who were age 100 or older. There were an estimated 340,000 at the time of publication. The article went on to discuss how "Their numbers are projected to grow at more than 20 times the rates of the total population by 2050, making them the fastest growing age segment."

We are finding out it's statistically possible we are living longer and more meaningful lives. Most people need their retirement money to last them 30, 40 and maybe even 50+ years. The retirement our grandparents prepared for is much different than what we need to prepare for. It's more critical than ever that we start to seriously understand and know what it is that we want our retirement life to look like and what we need to do in order to fulfill that vision.

This is the most important question I hear: What should every individual be doing now to eliminate outliving their savings? Learning to control spending and eliminating debt are two of the most important thing. You have many options for looking at and reducing your debt. But you have to start somewhere. This is the 6-point plan I share with all my clients.

1. Pull your credit report and make sure that you are aware of all your debt that's under your name. If you notice items that are not yours, make sure to bring it to the attention of your financial planner and the authorities.

2. Work on a debt elimination plan that clearly outlines current debt, repayment options and goals. Include your financial planner in the process and make sure you are holding yourself accountable to follow-through.

3. Reduce your expenses and learn to live within your means. This is often the most difficult choice for most individuals. However, I promise it pays off! Learning about needs versus wants can help you retire sooner and with more money. Think of the benefits!

4. Make sure you have a handle on what your lifestyle really costs. Necessities such as housing, utilities and food are important. You need to also budget and plan for hobbies, hair/spa treatments, lawn care and snow removal services, and more. Work with your financial planner to create a list of everything you'll need to address, so nothing is missed.

5. Make sure you are inflating your future expenses to see what your estimated retirement budget will be at the start of your retirement. Your income needs may grow during your retirement for things like food, medical bills, transportation and more.

6. Take monies above and beyond your emergency fund (three to six months of savings) into appropriate investments in order to keep up with the cost of inflation. Your money sitting in cash not earning

anything is actually costing you!

Myth #3: Retirees don't pay large amounts in taxes, or the burden is significantly smaller

The years before you retire tend to be your highest earning years which equate to your highest tax years. Often, children have moved out and expenses are lower because of this. I often find pre-retirees are not fully utilizing their employer sponsored plans to not only save more money, but drastically reduce their taxes. I often hear the following reasons as to why individuals are not taking advantage of their employer's qualified sponsored plans:

- They do not understand tax savings
- They believe if something happens to their company then their money is at risk
- They are not sure about the investment choices in their plan
- They are getting the full employer match so they do not think they need to put any additional money into the plan

When you retire your tax bracket will not necessarily be lower than when you were working. Often, clients will find themselves in the same tax bracket or higher. If you start to add up all the sources of your retirement income: Social Security, Pension Income, IRA or other Retirement Income (not including Roth IRA accounts,) Dividends & Interest & Capital Gains on non-retirement accounts, any part time earned income, etc., it can add up fairly quick. If you look at your expenses you will see what your income needs are. Just because you are retired does not necessarily mean your expenses go down, either. Often, I see clients increase their living expenses because they'd like to travel, participate in hobbies, and more. This may mean taking more distributions off retirement accounts which results in more taxes being due. Do not assume your tax bracket will fall just because you are retired.

Another issue I often see with retirement account distributions is the lack of awareness surrounding taxes. I often get asked what tax amount will be due on a distribution.

Whatever you pull from your accounts will be added to your income for the year. That means that you may go up a tax bracket. I always tell my clients they should consult their accountants in order to get a good gauge on what will be owed so we can withhold the proper amounts. While surprises are not good, withholding too much isn't either. Many people have the misconception getting a huge tax refund is free money.

A tax refund means you paid too much into the IRS. If you are retired and pulling off your retirement assets, then you are pulling money out that you did not need to pull. This money was not in your account working hard for you all year. Plus, because you pulled it out and it was taxed, you actually increased your taxes due. Having too high of a tax withholding can put you at risk of depleting your account. So stop thinking of tax refunds as "free money" or "a nice chunk of change to go blow" and start thinking about how it's sucking up your retirement future.

> **Hear It From An Expert:** When running a financial plan, your plan should take taxes into consideration. It isn't uncommon for a client to be surprised when they see what their income needs are in retirement once we add inflation as well as the estimated taxes they will withhold. This is especially startling to clients who have all their assets in qualified (retirement) accounts because we have to take more money out of their retirement accounts in order to pay taxes so this actually increases the income need on their plan.

Keep in mind, you do have to pay taxes on your IRA or other retirement account money after 59 ½. I often am told by a new client they won't have to pay taxes once they turn 59 ½ on their retirement distributions. It's a big misconception. At 59 ½ you no longer have a 10% penalty on your distributions, but you still have to pay income taxes. The amount you will pay depends on what your total income is. The more you take out of your account, the higher your tax bill. Distributions are considered ordinary income so each dollar you take out gets taxed. Having taxes withheld on your account means that your total distribution includes the money being withheld for taxes. So if you withdraw $20,625 and withhold $6,875 (or 25% for Federal and State taxes) you are being taxed on the full amount of $27,500 - not the $20,625 that you received. The tax money you have to withdraw can really eat away at your retirement nest egg.

Lastly, there is a big misconception you do not have to pay taxes on your Social Security Income, (SSI). While some people do not owe taxes on their SSI, I always tell my clients that you want to pay taxes on your SSI. Why is this? Well, the people who do not have to pay taxes generally are at the poverty level and only receive SSI. They have no other sources of income. For my clients who do have other sources of income, chances are they are going to have to pay. Depending on your income the IRS will tax your SSI between 50-85% of your total SSI check. So it's important to factor taxes on your SSI when doing retirement planning.

Mark and Vicky's Retirement Story:

Mark and Vicky first came to me because they were looking to retire anywhere from six months to two years out. Mark works for an automotive company and Vicky works for a technology company. Mark and Vicky had done a lot of things right – they were big savers. They had always lived within their means and had no debt.

Although Mark and Vicky had saved quite a bit of money, they were not utilizing their employer sponsored retirement plans to the fullest. Because of this, the $30,000 per year they were saving was costing them $12,000 per year in taxes. By maximizing both their plans by contributing the $17,500 per person allowed, plus an additional $5,500 catch up contribution they could each contribute since they are over 50, their savings could go from $30,000 per year, to $42,000 per year just by deferring it into their employer sponsored 401(k) plans.

Another issue Mark and Vicky had: they had their savings sitting in cash. We moved their savings, minus six months of expenses which we kept for emergency money, to a managed account which included investments in bonds, stocks and alternative investments.

Hear It From An Expert: Paying more in taxes than you have to can drastically reduce the amount of money you have in retirement. Finding a financial planner who can help you decipher and make sense of your employer plan can pay off big.

A note on big spending before retirement

Getting your big projects done before you retire can save you thousands in taxes. Need a new roof? Want to upgrade your boat? Have dental work you need done? Once you retire you have a fixed income and it is typically less than what you were making while working. Taking care of projects before you are retired by utilizing your excess surplus from your income is a great way to avoid paying the taxes, instead of pulling from your retirement account.

If you retire and have to sell off your non-retirement assets, chances are you will have to pay capital gains. If you take money out of your retirement accounts you will have taxes, unless it comes from a Roth IRA. Even if you do take it from a Roth IRA, you're reducing the earnings power of your Roth, which reduces your future tax free income.

While you are working, you may have better healthcare then once you retire. Getting dental work, vision or other surgeries done before you retire could allow you to save money once your deductible is fulfilled. Any out of pocket expenses are better paid with your work earnings vs. using your savings and retirement funds.

For large purchase items you know you will have to make in the first few years of your retirement, but don't need right now, (like a new car,) consider putting aside your cash surplus from your earned income.

Once you are retired, if you are able to split projects or big purchase items into different tax years you may save yourself quite a bit in taxes. Here's a great example:

Jeremy and Katie's Retirement Story:
Jeremy and Katie were in their third year of retirement. They decided that they wanted to add a pool to their vacation home. The $60,000 needed to accomplish this project was going to be taken out of their IRA's, since all of their savings were tied up in tax deferred IRA's. They were planning to take a distribution for the full amount in the current calendar year when they came in to see me. They were getting ready to leave to Florida where their vacation home is. They typically spend November through April in the Sunshine State and they were antsy to get the money into their account before they left.

After consulting with their CPA, I explained to them how taking $60,000 out of their IRA was going to throw them into a higher tax bracket. If they took all the money out in the current calendar year it was going to cost them an additional $40,000 in taxes. So their distribution of $60,000 now turned into $100,000. Jeremy and Katie were unaware how much they were going to lose in tax money. I asked them when the latest was that they needed the money by. Katie said nothing was in writing yet.

If they could wait until January, taking a distribution this year and the rest of the money January 1st, they would only pay $20,000 in taxes. So it would essentially save them half in taxes- $20,000!! After much discussion, Katie and Jeremy decided that they would use the clubhouse pool for another season, and hold off on their pool until the New Year. Smart move!

By splitting the distributions up into two calendar years, Jeremy and Katie saved a lot of money in taxes. The money they saved in taxes was still in the IRA continuing to grow. By doing a little bit of planning, they saved a lot of money and kept on track to meet their retirement goals.

Chapter 3
FINANCIAL PLANNING EXPOSED:
COMMUNICATION WITH YOUR FINANCIAL PLANNER

Myth #1: It's okay to hide information from your financial planner.

Myth #2: Your Financial Planner does not need to call you back in a timely fashion, and you don't need to call them back either.

Myth #3: It's okay to stay in the dark about how financial planning really works.

Myth #1: It's okay to hide information from your financial planner.

Let's say, you woke up this morning with a headache, that slowly evolved into a migraine, which in turn caused you to feel sick to your stomach for most the day. Tomorrow, when you wake up, you're going to go to the doctor, but, you're only sharing half your symptoms. Your doctor, ever the consummate professional, will certainly realize everything going on. This is the problem: When your doctor asks if you've had any stomach issues, if you say no, you risk a misdiagnosis. Financial planning is a bit like going to the doctor. Your planner needs to diagnose what's going right and wrong with your accounts. Not sharing all the symptoms of what you are experiencing can cause your planner to only hear half of what is going on. Since I've been in the business, I've learned to pick up cues when things are not exactly as they seem. When I notice something seems off, I always ask questions of my clients to determine if my gut instinct is correct. Being honest with your financial planner means sharing information even when you're embarrassed or worried. Remember your financial plan is based on the details of your situation. Hiding items, behaviors and accounts actually hurts your financial planning.

When I Fired A Client

Jana's Spending Story:

Jana was a multimillionaire who loved to spend money quickly. While going through divorce, it wouldn't be uncommon for Jana to spend over $6,000 a month on things, (clothes, purses, jewelry, etc.) In the last year alone, Jana went through a half-a-million dollars. Jana has a gorgeous wardrobe and accessories that would make even movie stars jealous, but Jana stopped sticking to her budget and financial plan.

I brought up the concern that Jana could outlive her money. She was clearly hiding debt from me and not making her payments.

I mentioned to my client, "Jana, are you sure you don't have any other credit cards, or accounts? I help you, I need to know all the accounts that are in place so I can add them to our financial plan and we can monitor progress."

Jana replied, "That's it!" Knowing Jana wasn't telling the whole truth, I had a difficult decision to make. I truly cannot help my client without her being transparent with me. Jana had brought up several times that she wanted to take out money from her IRA to finance trips and expensive luxuries. I explained the tax implications for taking money out of an IRA too soon, but Jana wasn't worried about the money. I wondered why she needed it to begin with, if she had enough to finance what she wanted to buy, see or do.

"I have lots of money. I'll pay a little more in taxes- so what?" Jana was adamant that she knew best. That day, I fired Jana as a client. It wasn't that I didn't want to help Jana- exactly the opposite! I wanted to have a great relationship with my client and with Jana refusing to be transparent about the full scope of her spending and financial situation, I understood that wasn't possible. The last I heard, Jana did indeed outlive her retirement funds and she's struggling to get by.

Hear It From An Expert: If you are hiding information from your planner, you are setting yourself up to be a victim in your own life. You are better than that. Don't set yourself up to fail.

Myth #2: Your Financial Planner does not need to call you back in a timely fashion and you do not need to call them back either.

This topic always baffles me. I'll be meeting with a new client and they will tell me they don't get calls back from their financial advisor/planner. It's not that it only occurred once, (everyone is human and mistakes happen) but it is a recurring issue clients easily overlook. I often hear:

"Well I assume they are busy"

"I think I'm not their most important client"

"I eventually get a call back after several attempts"

Your finances are important and the person you work with should be accessible and communicate with you every step of the way. When you enter into a financial planning relationship, please remember it takes care and concern from both sides. A client can't get help reaching his or her goals, if the financial planner has unanswered questions. This is why it's not ok for your financial advisor or planner to not communicate with you. While many issues can be handled by office staff, including, paperwork, income distributions, and scheduling- two way communication is vital. Your finances are simply your goals and dreams in the form of money. Would you want to miss out on an experience you've been looking forward to, because of communication issues? Why would you want to work with anyone who can't even return your phone call, or vice versa.

Here are three ways to become better with financial communication with your planner:

1.) I often make calls to my service provider's in-between appointments or when I'm on the road with my Bluetooth headset- especially return phone calls! If you are heading on a long trip, take time in the car to schedule appointments and make sure to bring information you may need for the call. If you aren't driving, you'll have the ability to take notes. If you are driving, you can always ask your planner to send you a summary of the action items from the call.

2.) As a mom, I know how difficult it is to add more to your plate. Between family and work, it seems there aren't enough hours in the day. As a woman, I understand the need to get away, relax and unwind. When most of my girlfriends think, "me time," they don't think about their financial planner- but they should! When you're

31

finances are in order, your life can become a lot less stressful! Schedule time on your calendar to go over the items you need to return to your financial planner, and write down a list of questions about money, investing and how your portfolio is doing. You'll be amazed at how much less stressful financial planning can become. You can encourage your friends to do the same.

3.) Ask for help with accountability. We're all busy professionals and adults. However, if we are honest with ourselves, we realize the things we don't like often slip away to make room for more of the things we enjoy. We can't do it all and recognizing we need an extra push is vital to being even more successful. Ask a spouse, girlfriend or child to remind you to get a follow-up call done and then celebrate when the task is completed! It'll help create a fun memory around your financial planning and allow you to have a special moment with those you care about.

Most professionals work 9 to 5. If you need to see a doctor, CPA, or an attorney you typically have to take time off work. For some reason, people seem to think they shouldn't have to take time off for their financial planning. It doesn't really make sense, does it? Your finances are a crucial part of your life. I understand having a crazy schedule. However, most people have a lunch break, so if you are finding it hard to see your financial planner and you don't want to take time off work, then you can always utilize the phone, or email, too.

I know that I often have phone appointments and /or face to face appointments with clients during the lunch hour. Sometimes it involves a three-way call so both spouses/partners are on the line, and sometimes it involves one spouse/partner face to face and the other on speaker phone for the pertinent information.

Hear It From An Expert: I hire talented professionals in my firm. Many times, a client's phone call can be addressed and any action needed can be completed by my team members. For the times that a client needs to speak directly with myself, my team will let the client know when I will be able to contact them back. Communication is valued in my firm and I always try my best to return phone calls within 24 hours. Often, a phone appointment will be scheduled accommodate my clients and avoid playing phone tag.

A Note on the Annual Review

At a minimum, you should be having an annual review with your financial planner. If you haven't heard from your financial planner/advisor or their staff, then you need to find a new firm to work with. It's just not ok to never hear from the firm you work with.

While I realize everyone is busier than ever, there are many ways to have an annual review. I have several clients who live out of state and when we aren't able to meet face to face, we have phone appointments. With the convenience and ease of secure email, it's easy to be able to send reports, etc. that we may want to look at. For clients who aren't internet savvy, we can always regular mail reports beforehand.

Make sure that you return your financial planner's call. They are calling you for a reason. They may need to make changes they can't make without your approval, or they may need additional information from you in order complete a goal in your portfolio. Not calling your financial planner or their staff back, means you aren't holding up your end of the relationship.

> **Hear It From An Expert:** If you want to meet your financial goals then make sure both you and your financial planner are making your goals a priority. At the very least a thorough review should be held annually, and there should be regular contact throughout the year whether it be your financial planner or their staff.

Myth #3: It's okay to stay in the dark about how financial planning really works.

Ladies and gentlemen, it's time we demystify and distance ourselves from the cult of, "financial stupidity." We all understand how money works. We can add, subtract, multiply and even in the right circumstances; we can find the value for, "x." However, financial planners aren't numbers gurus; we're simply knowledgeable about the financial markets, options, and landscapes. It's our job to help you navigate the often misunderstood world of retirement, savings, pensions and more. But, we can't do it alone. As a financial planner, I'm still stunned when a client doesn't want to take any responsibility to learn about their accounts, options, or financial decisions. I've heard a lot of, "you know best!"

While I do know about the market, best practices and what personally will be best for each individual, I still struggle speaking to adults who want nothing to do with their financial planning. It does not serve you to stay ignorant about the financial market. Furthermore, it doesn't help you to go to our neighbors, friends or family who don't understand all the implications of your situation. Ask the experts questions: We're here to help!

If your financial planner ever makes you feel stupid for a question you ask, it's time to find another financial planner. A good financial planner will allow you to:

> Ask questions in an open way and receive clear, helpful answers. Your financial planner should feel like they are in a partnership with you to achieve your goals and help motivate and inform you on how best to get to the finish line. If your financial planner doesn't have an immediate answer to a question, they should point you to resources that can help- both online and off. Finally, your planner should follow-up with answers in a timely manner and make themselves available, if needed.

I often hear:

> "My financial planner doesn't explain things so I can understand."

> "My financial planner just tells me not to worry about it because they will take care of me."

> "My financial planner gets defensive when I voice my concerns."

While you may not understand everything the first time around, you should have a general idea why you are doing what you are doing. If something doesn't make sense, please ask your planner to explain. If your planner has difficulty explaining why you're doing what you are doing, ask questions until you feel confident you have the right information and enough information to be on-board with the decision. If not, it may be time to look for a different financial planner.

True financial planning involves building a professional relationship with your planner. Just like any strong relationship, it involves communication and trust. You should feel comfortable asking questions, expressing concerns, and asking your financial planner to explain something again and again.

Financial planning can be an intense process. You probably won't remember every single detail. It's important you have a planner you feel comfortable working with and asking questions - no matter how hard those questions are.

While I realize that conflict is uncomfortable for most people, by expressing your concerns to your financial planner you give them the opportunity to explain something you may not understand, reveal information that you may not have at the tips of your fingers, or clear up any misconceptions.

Sylvia and Tyler's Financial Success Story:
I recently met with Sylvia and Tyler. They had been clients of mine for 10 years and we always had good communication. The past 18 months I kept telling my staff something must be wrong. They were no longer returning my calls, or my team members' calls. We had sent several letters telling them we were trying to contact them, but had heard not a peep.

They finally had responded to one of my team members calls and scheduled an appointment. When they came in they told me that they had not been calling back because they were unhappy with their returns. They had been comparing notes with their friends and it seemed that their friends had made more money because they had made everything back from 2008 and were up another 50%.

We pulled up all of their information from the last 10 years. We looked at the amount of money they had deposited, the amount of money they had taken out in distributions, and the annual return of each account.

Sylvia knew that she had taken some money out, but she didn't realize what a big percentage of her account it was. "I knew that you told me that I was taking too much out but I just didn't realize how much," she said after looking at her numbers.

Sylvia had taken over 78% of her principle amount out of her account over the last 10 years. She had 10% more than what her original deposit was, but she really had no idea how much she had already spent. She also had taken the majority of her money out when the market was down in 2008 for a deposit on her daughter's house, so it had affected the account even more.

When we looked at Tyler's account, he didn't even remember that he had ever taken any money out of his IRA.

Sylvia piped in, "That was from our trip to South America. And that was the year we did our addition on our cabin, and that was the trip we took our grandkids on…"

All of a sudden Tyler remembered taking money out of his account.

8 out of the 10 years they had invested with me they had double digit returns. I asked them if their returns looked bad.

"No," they both said and shook their head in unison.

"Are you still unhappy with your returns?" I asked.

They both said, "No".

"Ok, well we've missed out the last 18 months on a lot of growth because you didn't call me back and we had changes we wanted to make," I explained. I reviewed with them how I had discretion on two of their accounts but that the third account wasn't an account that I could make changes on without their permission.

"We were just unhappy, but I can see that we were not looking at the correct information," Tyler said.

"I understand, but we've been together 10 years. You know that I believe in open communication. Please make sure that if you ever have any questions or concerns that you call me right away. Not calling me has cost you money."

Both Sylvia and Tyler promised me they would call me next time they had any questions or concerns.

Hear It From An Expert: There are *no* stupid questions when it comes to your finances. You don't have to understand everything, but you do need to understand why you are making the choices you are making. If you want a strong financial plan, then you have to build and value the relationship. Communication from both parties is required.

Chapter 4
FINANCIAL PLANNING EXPOSED:
GIFTS, DONATIONS, AND SPOILING THE GRANDKIDS

Myth #1: It will be easy to say no when your family members come asking for money.

Myth #2: Retirees should donate the same amount in retirement that they did while working.

Your heart strings are attached to your family. It's not a surprise retirees often have a hard time saying no to their children and/or grandchildren and this is one of the biggest ways I see expenses creep up on retirees. Some people are good at setting limits, while others don't think about the consequences to their own financial situation.

Before you retire, sit down with your financial planner and spouse/partner, and set reasonable limits as to what you will allocate towards helping out your children or grandchildren, if needed. By setting your limit, you are able to say, "My financial planner said my money is all tied up. I'm so sorry but this is all I can offer you," if your children and/or grandchildren need more than what you are able to realistically afford.

What this will do is allow you to have an annual amount that is there for emergencies. While you may not need to tap into this each year, the years you do not utilize these funds will allow you to have higher amounts if needed in future years. This will also allow you to have a boundary of what you realistically can utilize to help out your family members should the need occur. Not having any boundaries on how you can financially help your family members is never a good idea.

What about those situations that pop up where a family member may need more financial help for a lifesaving medical situation, or another situation you just feel is extremely important to their wellbeing? By knowing your limit, you are able to go back to your financial planner, discuss what is needed, and work with them on how you can best help out. This may require reducing your luxury expenses for a year or longer, changing some of your goals, etc. However, being able to have all the information regarding your situation should result in a better outcome for you to make an educated decision verse making a financial decision and dealing with the consequences blindly.

One of the biggest pet peeves of mine is when a client calls me and tells me they need to withdraw funds in order to gift money to their children because their accountant or attorney told them to. While this strategy is needed and can work for some clients, 80% of the time a client is NOT in a position to do this without affecting their retirement and putting themselves at risk of outliving their money. Or, the amount they should be gifting or donating is much less than what their accountant or attorney is telling them.

Tim's Retirement Story:

Tim has been a client of mine for over a decade. Although he is a millionaire, you would never guess if you ran into him. His house is still furnished in 1960 orange furniture, his carpet is shag green, and he is one of the thriftiest people I've ever met. Unfortunately, Tim's children only contact him when they need money and he has a hard time applying his thrifty principles with them.

Over the last 12 years, I have seen Tim give his children over $350,000. He currently lives only on social security and doesn't take any money from his investment accounts except for his Required Minimum Distributions (RMD's) from his IRA accounts that the IRS requires him to take.

Tim recently came to talk with me because he just was put in a legal situation with a piece of land that he co-signed and gave the deposit on for his son. His son hadn't done any due diligence on the land he bought and the county was requiring him to pay for certain land improvements.

Since his son is very irresponsible with money, it's was no surprise to me he is filing bankruptcy. This resulted in the courts coming after Tim instead of his son since Tim is the one that holds all the assets. Tim just had to pay out $52,000 to the county the piece of land is a part of. In addition, he wrote a check to his attorney for $12,000 and the IRS for $8,500 for the capital gains he had to pay on the investments we sold to cover everything.

Over the years, I had asked Tim to allow me to work with him to create boundaries for his children's constant requests for money. In the past, Tim didn't really feel the need. This was the straw that broke the camel's back. Tim called me one day and said, "I'm ready to set those limits you keep talking about. Also, I need to change my beneficiaries on all my accounts and send you my new trust papers. I've written my son out of my trust."

Tim's lack of setting financial limits on his children led to him ultimately having no relationship with his son. His other five children all now have financial limits and while he still has a relationship with them, he doesn't talk or see his firstborn son. If Tim had set boundaries in the beginning, he may still have a relationship with his son.

Remember, limits and boundaries can keep you from ruining your relationships with the people you love the most. When we give often and generously, we can also decrease the meaning and importance of the gifts. Sometimes we need help saying, "No." When in doubt, blame your Financial Planner.

Myth #1: It will be easy to say no when your family members come asking for money.

You worked hard for your money and you saved it for your retirement. Your children and grandchildren have an opportunity to save for themselves while they are still of working age. Unless you don't want to have to go back to work or live with your children, make sure that you discuss with your financial planner the impact that gifting and donations will have on your portfolio.

Unforeseen expenses in retirement will happen, and gifting your assets too early in life could cause you to outlive your money. While reasons do exist to spend down your assets in order to qualify for Medicaid, working with your financial planner, accountant, and attorney should help you make the best decision about what action you should take. Setting realistic amounts and sticking within the budget can be part of your insurance policy not to have to move back in with your children someday.

The current gifting limit set by the IRS you can pass tax free for 2014 is $14,000. However, just because there is a gifting amount allowed doesn't mean you should be utilizing it. With estate taxes not being assessed on a deceased person's estate until after $5,340,000 per donor, (a married couple has $10,680,000) many people will not need to worry about money being passed to their children.

Before you retire, make a pact with your spouse/partner that you will not gift money or spend down your assets without consulting your entire team of professionals. If you do begin a gifting strategy, make sure you are reviewing this on an annual basis with your team as laws, account values, and other important details change year to year.

Sam and Marty's Retirement Story:

Sam and Marty came to me because they were running out of their money. They had been retired for 15 years, were in their 70's and had raised a family of 10. Although they had put all 10 of their children through college, they still managed to retire with $850,000 saved.

Sam was a stay at home mom and Marty was an engineer at General Motors. He retired with a pension and both Sam and Marty were receiving Social Security. They were conservative investors and surprisingly had not seen a huge drop in their portfolio like the stock market drop most of their friends experienced.

When I first sat down with Sam and Marty they told me about their 10 children and 28 grandchildren. I could tell that they had raised a good family and were also a close family. They vacationed twice a year with the entire family and every holiday was a big celebration.

After learning about Sam and Marty's family, work experience, and lifestyle, Marty told me they had come to see me because, "we are running out of money."

Marty handed his statement to me and I could see that the $850,000 of savings they retired with 15 years ago was now only worth $150,000! I was a little shocked at first, but once the conversation continued it was clear why their portfolio had dwindled so fast.

Sam and Marty were paying for *everything* for their family. Every vacation, meal out, gift, grandchildren's activity, etc. was paid for out of their retirement account. Additionally, because of their pension, social security, and the distributions from the retirement account, they were in a 40% tax bracket so they were paying a hefty amount to the IRS on top of the amount they were spending on their family.

The ironic thing about their situation was that their children all had good paying jobs and were savers like they had once been. They could afford to pay for the things that Sam and Marty had been paying for and would often offer.

It took a few meetings of going through Sam and Marty's income and expenses, discussing realistic retirement distribution amounts and also working with them to set limits on their annual budget for money spent on their family.

Since Sam and Marty had raised such a close family, we discussed having a family meeting with their 10 children to talk about what the new limits were and how they needed their help in making sure they made the necessary changes.

The family meeting worked. Sam and Marty set their new limits, communicated it to their family, and are now building their account back up.

I recently saw Sam and Marty and asked them if the changes were hard to make or if any of the children were upset. Sam told me, "It actually wasn't hard because our children have made us stick with the plan we set. It has reiterated to us that we raised really great kids. We aren't having any less fun or seeing them any less. It was a little strange allowing them to buy us a meal every now and then, but whenever we start to argue they just remind us that although they love us they don't want to have to live with us again...it's kind of the running joke now in our family!"

Hear It From An Expert: Gifting too soon may cause you to outlive your money. Working with your team of professionals can allow you to have a strategy that leaves a legacy for your beneficiaries without you having to rely on your beneficiaries to take care of you for the remainder of your life.

STOP SENDING THINGS

START SENDING MEMORIES

Gifting with Grandkids: 5 Great Ways to Think Outside the Wrapping Paper

Start Sending Memories: Give an item that can't be wrapped.

Kate's Gift Tradition:

In Kate's family, her significant other comes from a very wealthy background and extravagant gifts made the children happy, but Kate was convinced her kids didn't need such fancy things.

After her 1 year old received a power wheels and a check for $1k for a birthday, Kate decided to ask her mother-in-law, Suzanne, to start spending time - instead of spending money. Living in a small townhouse and as a saver herself, Kate knew if the gift-giving continued in this way, there wouldn't be the space for all the items. Suzanne understood and now sends a card or minimal gift and instead, sends memories. For Kate's son's second birthday, Grandma sent a special kid-proof photo album of family memories with special notes underneath and emailed a video of her singing to the birthday boy. It was one of the most special gifts Kate's son had; it helped create a stronger bond with grandma- while not draining her retirement savings.

Have a Conversation around Holidays: Sitting Down with your planner and deciding which is which

Doug and Laura's Gift Tradition:

Doug comes from a family of 8, which over the years has grown to almost 75 people. Gift giving can be extremely expensive. Doug's wife, Laura loved Christmas, but knowing they couldn't give each niece, nephew or cousin a gift broke her heart. Holidays are stressful, especially for those on a fixed retirement budget. I worked out a plan with Doug and Laura that made all 75-people happy. We created a list of all the Holidays that Doug and Laura wanted to be able to provide gifts for. The list was enormous! In pairing down, Laura realized that while birthdays and Christmas were special, she could always send a card. And, it turned out that Laura really loved Halloween. So, instead of going all-out during Christmas or birthdays, Laura sent cards and during Halloween, she sent candy. It was still special and economical. The grandkids, nieces and nephews loved the thoughtful gifts and cards.

Start a Tradition: Sending something special instead of something new

Patty's Gift Tradition:

Patty's grandkids are all pretty close and love coming to her house. Patty is a fantastic baker and always is making some sort of treat. One day, Patty got the idea that she was going to start a new tradition.

Patty sent invitations to all of her grandchildren to come be a part of a bake off. Along with the invitation to spend the night was a $25 VISA gift card with instructions. The instructions told the grandkids that they were to go to the store and buy whatever candy, ice cream, etc, they wanted for the bake off. Any remaining money could be used to buy a Christmas movie or music.

Patty's grandkids all showed up with their goodies. Patty had a day of baking and creating new treats with her grandkids. When they weren't baking their grandkids played games, watched movies and listened to music. While Patty told me that she was pretty exhausted after her slumber party, it was the best memories of her grandkids she ever had! Her grandkids were still talking about their Christmas sleepover at grandma's and all wanted to know what the date was for the next holiday!

Give an Heirloom: Ensure something stays in the family by gifting it in a special way

Roy's Gift Tradition:

Roy has been a client of mine for about 10 years. He is a widower and has four grandchildren that he is close with. His one grandson he is especially close with and he usually spends a little more on him. We were watching his budget because of some unexpected medical bills this year.

Roy came in for his annual meeting and told me that he wanted to give his grandson something extra special for his 16th birthday and he had been thinking all year about what to do without ruining the new budget we had set for him. I half expected him to tell me that he did something foolish like buy him a car he couldn't afford.

Instead, Roy told me that one of the things he enjoys most is going hunting with his grandson. For his 16th birthday, Roy gave him an antique gun that had been in the family for 100 years.

Roy took out some pictures of him and his grandson with the gun. The smiles on both of their faces were priceless. This gift was something his grandson would always treasure and it didn't require him to blow up his budget. A win-win for all!

Myth #2: Retirees should donate the same amount in retirement that they did while working

A big discussion I often have with clients regards donations. Many of my clients follow tithing rules of their religious organizations. Often, they ask me what the rules are for retired members. I always tell them to talk with their religious leaders.

If you follow tithing rules, talk with your religious leader *before* you retire. Make sure that you let your financial advisor know what your requirements are and what you wish to follow once you retire.

Many clients of mine have been able to count their time and talent towards tithing once they are retired. Since retirees are on fixed incomes, it makes sense that many religious organizations have these policies.

Once you are retired, you may find that you wish to volunteer more for your religious organization that you are a member of. You may also be able to utilize your talents to help raise funds, solve issues or problems your organization faces, etc. Some organizations will actually allow members to count these hours towards part of their tithing requirements.

Make sure that you discuss with your financial planner which non-profit organizations you wish to support and what kind of monetary amount you wish to give. If you wish to leave money to one or more organizations, talk to your financial planner. Your financial planner should be working with a team of other professionals - such as an estate attorney and CPA- who can help create a strategy for gifting either during your lifetime or upon your death. If you are married or have people you wish to take care of after your death, but want remaining assets to be donated, your financial planner and other team members can design a plan suited to your wishes.

> **Hear It From An Expert:** If you plan on gifting or donating then you should be consulting your financial planner before any checks are written. Examining tax strategies, the impact on your overall financial situation, and other issues that need to be looked at *before* you gift or donate can help prevent you from outliving your money.

Chapter 5
FINANCIAL PLANNING EXPOSED:
SOCIAL SECURITY AND INSURANCE

Myth #1: Everyone is entitled to Social Security.

Myth #2: Pull your Social Security as soon as you can.

Myth #3: Your Social Security benefit can only be what is on your statement.

Myth #4: Insurance is all the same.

Have you ever really thought about how you will get income in retirement? Do you have a clear grasp on how social security works, how you distribute money out of your retirement and other saving accounts, pensions, etc.? Social Security is one of the biggest sources of the average American retiree's income. Yet, American's know little about how Social Security works, tax implications, and ways to draw from it.

The Social Security Administration used to send statements out each year. In order to save money they decided to stop mailing statements unless you are age 60 or older. In 2014, the Social Security Administration amended their policy again. If you are working, not receiving benefits, and have not registered for a My Social Security online account, you will receive statements about three months before your birthday at the following ages: 25, 30, 35, 40, 45, 50, 55, and 60. After age 60 you receive a statement each year.

In order to look at your personal information, you should go to www.ssa.gov. You can create a User ID and pull up your statement and run an estimate. This is an important step of your retirement planning!

Your statement is an important piece of your overall social security income. Page three of your statement lists all the years you have reported earned income. This is wages, business income, etc. Make sure that the correct earnings have been reported. If you find errors you should contact the Social Security Administration and have your correct earnings entered.

Your benefit is based on the top 35 years of income you have earned. So if you have 40 years of earnings, the five lowest years of earnings will be deleted. If you do not have 35 years, $0 will be entered into your calculation in order to determine your benefit.

Myth #1: Everyone is entitled to Social Security.

A big misconception is that everyone is entitled to Social Security. Unfortunately, this isn't the case. In order to receive a benefit, you must have earned 40 credits, which is equivalent to roughly 10 years of working. It's important that you know if you have the 40 credits or not. Your credits also count towards receiving Medicare at age 65 or if disabled. A good resource on Medicare qualification is located at: http://www.ssa.gov/pubs/EN-05-10043.pdf.

Gabriela's Social Security Story:
My good friend Gabriela recently came to see me. She is an American citizen but was born in Brazil. She moved to the USA a few decades ago with her husband but after 8 years got divorced.

We started discussing Social Security and she did not know what she had in credits. After talking with Social Security, it was determined that Gabriela only had 26 credits and needed another 14 (or roughly 3.5 years). Since she was not married at least 10 years, she does not qualify for a spousal benefit either.

Gabriela worked as an employee making approximately $75,000 per year before she left to start her own business. Over the last 4 years she has been deducting all of her business expenses for a loss. By not deducting all of her expenses and claiming a small amount, she can earn credits and become eligible.

In the year 2014, you must earn $1,200 in covered earnings to get one Social Security or Medicare work credit and $4,800 to get the maximum four credits for the year.

Source: http://www.ssa.gov/retire2/credits1.htm

Source: http://www.ssa.gov/pubs/EN-05-10072.pdf

By the time she is 60 she will have her 40 credits and be eligible to collect either her own benefit, or a spousal benefit, if she starts to claim the above amounts. While she will have to take a tax hit in the short term, the long term benefits greatly outweigh the short term tax liabilities each year.

Other clients I have who have had this issue have gone out and gotten part or full time jobs. I see this often with female clients as they may have been stay at home moms or taken significant time off to care for children or parents.

Spousal Benefits and Nonqualifying Spousal Benefits

If both spouses have earned 40 credits, they are entitled to take either their own benefit or ½ the amount of their spouses benefit. Pulling a spousal benefit does *not* reduce your spouse's benefit.

If one spouse qualifies for a benefit and the other spouse does not have enough earned credits for their own benefit, the no qualifying spouse can collect a spousal benefit from the qualifying spouses benefit as long as they have been married at least one year to the qualifying spouse, or if they are the parent of their child.

Source: http://www.socialsecurity.gov/retire2/yourspouse.htm#sb=2

> **Hear It From An Expert:** Know how many credits you have and to make sure your earnings are reported correctly.

A note on Social Security taxes

Another big misconception with Social Security is that once you start pulling retirement income that you don't have to pay taxes on it. I always tell my clients that you *want* to pay taxes on your social security income. Typically, the people who do *not* pay taxes are living on social security income only. And with the average paycheck being $1,294 per month*, it doesn't fare well for most retirees. Based on your total income and your filing status, you can have either 50% or 85% of your social security retirement income taxed.

* http://www.ssa.gov/news/press/basicfact.html

Hear It From An Expert: Make sure you factor in taxes when doing retirement planning if you plan on having other sources of income in retirement.

Myth #2: Pull your Social Security as soon as you can.

I often receive phone calls from retirees who want to know if they should pull their social security at 62, their full retirement age, or at 70. What they usually say is, "My friend told me that as soon as I can pull it, I should." Time and time again, I try to remind my clients the advice-giver doesn't understand all the details involved in social security.

For me to be able to give advice on social security, I need to pull an entire financial plan and understand what other income sources, expenses, assets, and debts, exist in my client's lifestyle. I also ask them if they are still working and if so what kind of income they have.

If you plan on working before you turn your full retirement age, then you need to be aware that there are limits as to how much you can earn before you get penalized. In 2014, for every $2 you earn above $15,480 you will have $1 reduced from your income check. *

If you reach full retirement age during 2014, we must deduct $1 from your benefits for each $3 you earn above $41,400 until the month you reach full retirement age. *

* http://www.ssa.gov/pubs/EN-05-10069.pdf

I usually hear grumbles when I tell individuals this. The good news is if you are still working past your full retirement age, you can earn as much as you want and still collect without having any benefits deducted.

It is also important to note that you are only penalized on earned income – this does not include pension income, retirement or other saving incomes.

There are other deciding factors about when to pull and how to pull involve myth #3, so keep reading…

Hear It From An Expert: If you pull your benefit at 62, it will be reduced. If you wait till age 70 before pulling, you will have a higher benefit. Waiting past 70 does not have any benefit.

Myth #3: Your Social Security benefit can only be what is on your statement.

When both spouses have worked and earned enough credits to qualify for Social Security benefits, several strategies exist in order to maximize benefits. Retirees are often unaware of the following strategies.

1. Claim Now, Claim More Later
    This strategy involves the spouse with the lower benefit claiming, and the spouse with the higher benefit only pulling a spousal benefit. This enables the spouse that has the higher benefit to receive some money now, let their benefit continue to grow, and then claim a higher benefit in a few years.

2. File and Suspend
    This strategy involves the spouse with the higher benefit filing, but immediately suspending. Doing this allows the spouse to claim a spousal benefit while the suspended benefit continues to grow.

3. File and Suspend + Claim Now, Claim More Later
    This is a combination of the two benefits above.

One of the best pieces of literature I have seen was written by AARP on these three strategies. Please reference the following hyperlink to see more information on who this works best with, more details on how to qualify, etc.

http://www.aarp.org/content/dam/aarp/money/budgeting_savings/2012-02/How-to-Maximize-Your-Social-Security-Benefits-AARP.pdf

Your financial planner should be able to run comparisons utilizing these strategies, as well as the listed benefits on your social security statement. Before you pull your social security, it pays to look at all your options and see how to maximize what you've earned.

Divorced Singles

I often work with clients who have been divorced. It comes time to draw social security and they either aren't aware they can pull off of their ex-spouses benefit, or they believe their ex-spouse will receive less money if they do so.

If you were married for at least 10 years and haven't gotten remarried, you are entitled to a spousal benefit. This works just like if you were still married – you receive 50% of what your ex-spouse is receiving. This does not decrease your ex-spouses income. Also, your ex-spouse can be remarried and you still are entitled to this benefit. It's also possible for your ex's new spouse to pull a full spousal benefit, even if you are.

In order to receive a spousal benefit from an ex-spouse your ex-spouse *must* have filed to receive a benefit. If your spouse is using either of the strategies listed above, you are able to pull a benefit.

If your ex-spouse hasn't filed for a benefit, you may start your benefit and then switch to a spousal benefit once your ex-spouse has filed. Knowing what your ex-spouse's benefit will be is important to discuss with your financial planner.

Widow Benefits: Mallory's Story:
If your spouse dies, you are entitled to widow's benefits as soon as age 60. However, you really need to consult with your financial planner because not every widow should pull benefits at age 60.

Meet Mallory. I met Mallory shortly after her husband died. Mallory was looking for financial guidance and had not yet started pulling social security. She was 60 and eligible to pull a widow's benefit, but something was stopping her from filing. "My other friends who are widows all tell me that I need to file for my widow's benefit but something is telling me that maybe I shouldn't," she told me.

"I'm glad you haven't. From what you told me so far, you would be penalized and your benefits would be reduced." Mallory looked at me confused.

Mallory was a business owner. She had wages and profits from her business that all flowed onto her tax return. I explained to Mallory that if you pull social security benefits before your full retirement age (Mallory's was 66) that after a certain income point that they will reduce your income benefits. Looking at what her income would, it would completely wipe out her widow's benefit.

The other bad part of Mallory pulling now was the benefit would no longer grow. She didn't need the income now and pulling her benefit was only going to increase her tax burden, eliminate what she should be getting, and give her a smaller lifetime amount.

Mallory decided not to pull her benefit and it is continuing to increase every year that she waits. Until she no longer receives earned income, or reaches her full retirement age, it just doesn't make sense.

Hear It From An Expert: Don't listen to your friends unless they are your financial planner. Everyone's situation is different.

Myth #4: Insurance is all the same.

Oh the dreaded word: Insurance! It's a topic that no one really wants to talk about, including finance professionals! Having a conversation about what is going to happen when you die, become disabled or need to go into a nursing home isn't even fun to bring up. That's why a lot of financial advisors avoid it.

Financial planners look at your risks. While they can't predict exactly what will happen, financial planners can assess what kind of financial needs you and your family may have if one of the three scenarios above occurs. It involves a lot more than a quick calculation on a computer but getting a proper assessment so you know how much you should be insured for, as well as which type of insurance you should buy, is one of the ways your financial planner becomes even more valuable to you.

It's not a secret that insurance can be costly. I see many people avoid purchasing insurance because they believe it isn't necessary. But this is the thing - you wouldn't dismiss purchasing insurance on your home or automobile. However, your life, your health, and your income are extremely important to not only you but those that depend on you. Getting a proper assessment, obtaining the correct amount of coverage, and reviewing your insurance needs on an annual basis with your financial planner is important.

I've seen more retirees run out of their money because of disability, a long term care need, or the death of a spouse. I've also seen retirees run out of their money because they are pulling too much off of their investments in order to pay for insurance they don't need. These are often *preventable* situations. So let's breakdown the basics of the three insurances and discuss why you may need it and what type you may need.

Hear It From An Expert: Order an in-force illustration on your life insurance policy to bring to your next meeting with your financial planner. An in-force illustration shows greater details and will give your planner more background into understanding your policy and premiums.

Permanent vs. Term Life Insurance

Permanent life insurance is any policy that has cash value. Term insurance has an expiration date and no cash value. One of the easiest ways to think about term insurance is to think about how your auto insurance works. If you get into an accident then your coverage and benefits kick in. Your policy expires every 6 months, or year, unless you renew it. With term insurance, if you die, the policy pays the death benefit. You choose a set period of time to be insured for the same annual cost. Typical terms are 10, 15, 20, 25, 30 and even 40 year policies.

If you have a permanent insurance policy, you should order an in force illustration once a year. This is much different than your life insurance statement. When you first see your in force illustration, it may look like nothing to you. An in force illustration will have many columns of numbers. For many people it is overwhelming.

If you take this to your financial planner, they can use the illustration to show you what is happening with your policy. Many policies were sold as "lifetime policies" but the insurance agent never explained to the client that your policy is typically based on a hypothetical rate of return. If your policy hasn't earned at least that rate, you could be in jeopardy of losing your policy.

I've seen many clients have policies that were originally set up to earn 12% or higher. They bought these policies in the 80's when interest rates were really high. Because the policies have not earned at least 12%, they are at a risk of losing their policy.

The clients either need to add more money into the policy, let their policy lapse, or do a 1035 exchange into a new contract.

The good news is that over the years our life expectancy has gone up. Because of this, insurance costs have actually gone down for many people even though they are older.

The bad news is that some individuals have more health issues and can no longer get good ratings or even insured.

Having a life insurance review *before* you retire will allow you to truly know what amount of money you should be spending on life insurance. You don't want to retire and all of a sudden be told that you need to pay more money into your policy or you will lose your coverage.

Jamie's Life Insurance Story:

Jamie was a new client. We were going through her confidential profile and started talking about her life insurance. From the in force illustration, it was very clear that she was going to either have to start putting in an additional $2,300 per year, or she would lose her coverage in the next three years.

Jamie had no idea that her policy was at risk. She only ordered the in force illustration because it was on the supporting document list of our confidential profile. She told me that she had met with her agent when she got the policy and had never heard from him again. Unfortunately, this is not an uncommon scenario.

Jamie was planning on retiring in six months. She had been a single parent most of her child's life. Her husband died when her daughter was only five. Her daughter had been born mentally handicapped and Jamie had taken out the policy to help support her daughter's ongoing medical needs.

After a full assessment of Jamie's insurance needs, we determined that she needed an additional $350,000 of coverage. After putting the case out for quotes, we found a carrier that would allow us to do a 1035 tax free transfer of the cash value in her current policy. Because Jamie was in good health, she got a preferred rating and we were able to give her the total amount of insurance she needed. A no lapse policy that would guarantee her coverage through age 105 was chosen.

We also decided to add more to the policy in the next two years. Jamie decided that she would remain at her employer part time so we could then reduce what she needed to pay once she was fully retired in two years.

Another thing we did for Jamie was refer her to a trust attorney. Working with the trust attorney we were able to create a trust for her daughter and name the owner of the life insurance policy the trust. We were also able to direct who would manage the money upon Jamie's death.

Hear It From An Expert: Just because you think you have something, doesn't mean you do. Reviewing your situation on an annual basis helps to make sure that nothing is left unturned.

Life Insurance Cash Value

Life insurance that has cash value can be a way to receive income before 59 ½. It's important that you consult with your financial planner before you do this so you don't have tax implications.

When you have cash value on your life insurance policy, you are able to take tax free loans from it. You are not required to pay it back, however, it will create interest being charged to your cash value and will also lower your overall death benefit.

It is really important you have your financial planner run a full analysis of how a lower death benefit would impact your family should you utilize the loan feature on your cash value. It is also important to discuss the current interest rate that your policy will charge and to also look at an in force illustration (not a statement) on how this will impact your policy going forward both if you make payments towards the loan and if you don't make payments.

As you can see, if you retire early, different accounts have different pros and cons. Your financial planner can look at your entire financial situation and coordinate a strategy for you that allows you to keep the most and give the IRS the least.

Long-term Care

Long-term care insurance refers to a wide range of medical, personal and social services. This insurance gives you financial help with care that could involve home health care, adult day care, or nursing home care. This insurance is one way to subsidize the rising costs of long-term care and could potentially cover all or some of the expenses associated with home health care, or a facility. Most plans cover $50 - $250 worth of care, per day. However, in discussing with my clients, I often bring up a few key points to remember when selecting long-term care coverage:

Do the benefit amounts increase with inflation? Do you need to have a policy that will pay 100% of the costs, or only a partial amount? Do you want to lock in the premium cost and pay over several years or do you want a policy that is a pay for life? Does your policy allow for in home care or only a nursing home? These are just some of the questions your financial planner should review with you.

You'll need to make your financial planner aware of the type of long-term care policy you have or want so they may better budget your retirement dollars.

If you don't currently have a long term care policy, it's important to review your risks and look at scenarios of what would happen to your assets should you need this type of care. Not everyone should buy long term care insurance and that is why it's important to discuss your particular needs with your financial planner.

Disability

Disability is to replace a portion of your income should you no longer be able to work. It typically will pay out 60-70% of your income for a certain period of time or throughout life, depending on the policy you purchase. Policies that pay for life are often more expensive and due to this reason, most disability policies stop paying once the insured reaches age 65.

With that being said, make sure you understand the age limits of your policy. Most policies will not pay benefits out past age 65 - however, the insurance company will not necessarily stop billing you.

Jessica's Disability Story:

Jessica had been referred to me. She was in her 40's, single, owned her own business, and was responsible for taking care of her mother. Her mom was 74 and worked part time for Jessica doing some clerical work.

We were meeting for the first time and discussing her confidential profile. When we got to the disability portion, I asked why she was paying over $5,000 per year for her disability when her coverage was so low.

"It's actually for both my mother and I. I wanted to make sure if anything ever happened to her that she would be taken care of," Jessica said.

"Did your insurance agent tell you that most policies don't pay out any benefits after age 65?" I asked her.

"That can't be right. We bought the coverage when my mom was 68. Surely he would have told me that if that was the case," she said.

"I think you need to check on that. Why don't you write that down on your list and give him a call as soon as you get a chance." I suggested.

"Can we call him now?" Jessica asked.

"Sure." I replied and handed her the phone.

Jessica called her insurance agent and put it on speakerphone. She explained that she was working on financial planning with me and that I was questioning at what age benefits would stop being paid out.

"65," her insurance agent said.

"Then why have I been paying thousands of dollars for six years on my mother who was 68 when I first acquired coverage?" Jessica asked.

The insurance agent got very quiet. Finally he said, "Well you have a group policy through your business so it's up to you to verify which of your employees are eligible and which aren't."

As you can imagine, the conversation proceeded to get a little ugly. Jessica was fuming. She asked for her money back and the insurance agent said that he would need to get back with her.

At the time of writing this, it has now been 18 months and Jessica is still fighting with the insurance company. She has paid out over $20,000 to the insurance company for her mother to receive a benefit that she would never have been able to use. She currently has an arbitration date scheduled and I'm hoping that she can be refunded.

When bought and used correctly, disability can prevent a family from financial ruin. Brian's story is the exact opposite of Jessica's.

Brian's Disability Story:

Brian was a single dad of twin 12 year old boys. The boys' mother was out of the picture and Brian received no support from her. He was working in his garage on his classic car one day and his car literally fell on top of him. One of his son's was in the garage with him and called 911. He passed out before the ambulance came. When he woke up he was in the hospital and his arm was in a cast from his shoulder to his fingers.

Brian was looking at years of reconstructive surgery and rehabilitation. From age 43 to 46 he was unable to work. Fortunately, Brian had a disability policy that paid out 65% of his wages. He also was able to obtain Social Security Disability. The two income sources combined enabled him to keep his house, his car and pay the medical bills he had. It literally saved him from financial ruin and allowed him to continue to put food on the table for his two boys.

Brian's employer was able to rehire him when he was able to work again. The boys were no longer 12 but were just about to turn 16. Brian was able to go back to work and called me to tell me that he was looking for a car to buy them as a surprise for their 16th birthday.

Brian was lucky. He had coverage when he needed it.

Hear It From An Expert: Your actions that you take now will have a lifetime of consequences not just for you, but for other people who rely on your income and assets. Obtaining a proper illustration of how much and what kind of coverage can save you from financial disaster.

A Note on Medicare

Before you retire, make sure your financial planner is adding a figure for your future medical costs and inflating that number throughout your life expectancy. If you have existing health issues, or a family history of certain conditions, discussing this with your financial planner is important. Remember, the more information you give your financial planner, the better equipped they are to help you prepare for the future. Medical is a *big* unknown.

One of the hardest things we try to anticipate with clients is how much medical will cost them. With the average 65 year old who is on Medicare paying an additional $5,000 out of pocket, the costs of medical continuing to rise, and no clear understanding of how Obamacare is going to impact the retirement landscape, a retirees healthcare costs are a big, "what if."

One of the biggest surprise expenses I have clients withdrawing more money for is dental. I can't tell you how many times I've gotten a call about a root canal or denture expense, and it isn't a cheap expense. Many times a client will have a dental bill in the thousands and they typically are withdrawing it from their retirement account which means they also have to pay taxes on their distribution. Unsurprisingly, health care costs seem to start off relatively low and get higher as a retiree ages. And many things aren't covered.

I've had clients not have cancer treatments, dialysis, hip and knee replacements, and other medical costs be covered. Its mind blowing how life saving treatments such as cancer treatment or dialysis cannot be covered but that is the reality that we live in. Furthermore, treatments aren't cheap.

Medicare 101: Myth vs. Fact

Myth: If you need a nursing home Medicare pays for it

Medicare does *not* pay for nursing homes. In all reality, Medicare is basically a hospitalization policy. When you turn 65, you have to opt into Medicare. There many different supplemental policies that retirees have to choose from. Even after you purchase your supplemental policy, there are still a lot of things it doesn't cover. It's confusing to say the least.

Myth: Medicare is welfare

Medi*caid* is welfare. You have to be eligible financially for Medicaid.

Medi*care* is what an eligible 65 year old receives and it is *not* welfare. However, as stated above Medicare is basically hospitalization and many rules exist in order to maximize your benefits. Please reference the hyperlink for more information: http://www.medicare.gov/what-medicare-covers/

Myth: Medicare pays for your doctor visits.
Again, this is false. Medicare is mostly just a hospitalization policy and that is why you need a supplemental policy.

Myth: Medicare covers prescriptions.
False. An add-on to your supplemental policy gives you a prescription plan. This is your Part D plan but it doesn't mean you won't have any out of pocket costs for your prescriptions.

Lewis' Medicare Story:
Lewis worked at Chrysler and was offered a buyout when he was 55. He took the buyout, received his money, and came to see me in order to invest the proceeds.

After running a plan, it was clear that Lewis should *not* have taken the buyout. He received $350,000 in a lump sum rollover. He only had $150,000 saved in his 401(k) and another $20,000 in non-retirement assets. Before taking the buyout, his income was $75,000 per year.

If Lewis had worked another 7 years, he would have been able to receive $2,500 per month with full medical benefits. He also could have pulled an income from social security, to supplement the $2,500 per month. He could have utilized his $70,000 of salary money over the next 7 years to increase his 401(k) contributions and reduce his existing debt to zero.

Because Lewis took the buyout, he lost his medical insurance. (Please note that this is not the case for all pension buyouts or lump sum rollovers – please check with your pension department for your specific details.) The only way to avoid taxes on his pension lump sum buyout was to roll it to an IRA. Any money he took out between now and 59 ½ would be subject to a 10% penalty and ordinary income taxes unless Lewis decided to do a 72T Distribution till he was 60. The problem was, the 72T didn't offer enough income for him to pay his bills so he had to take all of his distributions with the 10% penalty plus ordinary income tax.

Lewis and Pam were retired for only three years when Lewis' kidney started to fail him. They had reduced their expenses the best they could, but they were pulling 18% off their accounts each year, which was much more than the recommended 4-5%.

Their assets had greatly depreciated due to this. Also, the year before Lewis was diagnosed with a failing kidney he had changed his medical insurance in order to reduce his premiums. Unfortunately, the new policy that he signed up for didn't cover the majority of the dialysis bill.

Lewis started going to dialysis three times a week. At $125 a pop out of pocket, the medical bills ramped up quickly. He is waiting for a kidney and has been on dialysis for two years now. He has racked up $40,000 in credit card bills that are in both Lewis and Pam's name. If Lewis dies, Pam will still be responsible for this credit card debt since it is in her name. The money between Lewis and Pam has been depleted to $85,000. Unfortunately, Lewis and Pam are on track to outlive their income.

Remember: *Before* you take a buyout and retire, consult your financial planner to make sure that your financial plan has medical expenses factored in. Before changing any medical insurance, make sure you know what it covers. Consulting a qualified health insurance agent is recommended.

Hear It From An Expert: Maximizing Medicare benefits can be tricky. For example, if you want your Part A to be maximized, then you must be admitted to the hospital and not just be "under observance". To read more about this topic visit http://www.shardfinancial.com/admitted-vs-under-observation-what-you-dont-know-can-cost-you-thousands/.

Wills, Trusts, and Powers of Attorney

It is really important you make sure your estate plan documents are up to date. While a will is only good once you are dead, a trust may or may not be effective during your lifetime. Powers of Attorney for both your medical and financial affairs need to be up to date. If you are alive and cannot make decisions on your medical or financial issues, having an up to date Power of Attorney for both medical and financial is necessary. Don't assume that your spouse can make decisions for you in this type of a situation. Without proper documents, your spouse can not make medical decision or utilize assets that are in just your name, this includes retirement accounts and bank accounts while you are alive.

If you had your estate plan created five years ago or longer, it's time to see an attorney and have a review. Many laws have changed that require documents to be updated. Not having documents updated could make your current documents invalid.

Chapter 6
FINANCIAL PLANNING EXPOSED:
YOUR RETIREMENT PLAN INCOME AND TAXES

Myth #1: All retirement accounts are created equal.

Myth #2: If a strategy exists, you should use it.

Myth #3: If your friend is doing something, then you should too.

Myth #4: It's an easy choice whether to take a pension rollover or buyout.

457	401k	IRA Traditional Simple SEP	Roth IRA
Under 59½ Ordinary Income Taxes	10% Penalty + Ordinary Income Taxes	10% Penalty + Ordinary Income Taxes	10% Penalty and Ordinary Income Taxes On Gains (No Taxes on Principal/Cost Basis)
Over 59½ Ordinary Income Taxes	Ordinary Income Taxes	Ordinary Income Taxes	Tax Free If Held At Least 5 Years

Myth #1: All retirement accounts are created equal.

Luke's Story:

Luke was 58, was being laid off and knew to call me. "They are laying me off and I negotiated a great deal for severance, but I remember that we had a conversation once about if I left my employer before 59 ½ that I needed to do something. I can't remember what it was though…"

"When is your last day?" I asked. Luke had 30 days. "Ok. We need to roll some of your IRA money into your existing 401(k)." I told Luke. "If you need money between now and 59 ½, you can pull it from your 401(k) without a 10% penalty. You will still have to pay taxes but you won't have the added penalty."

"I don't think I'll need it," Luke told me.

"You have $15,000 in emergency money and all the rest of your money is in retirement accounts. We need to roll some over just in case," I told him.

We immediately got going and moved his money over so we had some funds to utilize in case he did need funds in the next 18 months. Luke called me about four months into his retirement. "Guess what? I need $10,000 - my roof is leaking everywhere! I spent my emergency money on a new transmission and bought myself a new hunting gun the day I retired. I just don't have any left."

All of Luke's assets were in his retirement accounts. "Let's call your 401(k) company then," I told him. "This is exactly why we rolled some money from your IRA into your 401(k) before you left. You will have to pay taxes, but we can avoid the 10% penalty."

Luke took a distribution and avoided a 10% additional tax because of simply moving his money from one account to another before he retired.

Hear It From An Expert: Knowing the rules of different accounts can be confusing. The best way to make sure that your assets are where they should be is to sit down with your financial planner and go over your options.

Non-Retirement Accounts (excluding Non-Qualified Annuities)

Let's start first with non-retirement accounts. This could be cash in saving or checking accounts, certificates of deposit (CD's), stocks, bonds, mutual funds, or exchange traded funds (ETF's).

If you have money in these types of investments then you are probably earning some type of dividend or interest. During the years that you are trying to grow your money, investors typically reinvest the dividends and interest. Even though you are reinvesting this money and don't receive a check, you get a 1099 each year that reports everything to the IRS so you can pay taxes. Since you are already paying taxes on this money, you could turn off the reinvestment option on your investments and start receiving the dividends and interest in the form of income.

Selling shares may also be an option for you if needed. Before doing any of this, consult your financial planner and accountant so you understand the tax ramifications. Typically, investments held longer than a year will qualify for long term capital gains. Holdings of less than one year will qualify for short term capital gains.

If you have a good financial planner and accountant working together on your financial decisions, they will be able to coordinate what is sold. Offsetting some capital gains with losses can help reduce your current income tax liability. Losses that are from past years that you can roll forward should be taken into consideration as well.

Non-Qualified Annuities (Non retirement accounts)

Non-qualified annuities have a 59 ½ rule. Any money you put into annuities is your cost basis and will be considered a tax free event as a return of principal. Any gains you earn will have a 10% tax penalty plus taxes if you take money out before 59 ½.

The way non-qualified annuities work is on a last in, first out tax schedule. What this means is the earnings will come out first. So you have to get through all your earnings before you pull out the principle, or non-taxed part.

Do not confuse a non-qualified annuity with an annuity that is bought inside your IRA. Annuities bought inside IRA's will fall under IRA tax guidelines.

457

If you have a 457 account, you can pull money out without a 59 ½ tax penalty. So utilizing your 457 may be more advantageous than other retirement accounts if you retire before 59 ½. You still will have to pay ordinary income taxes on your distributions.

401(k)'s

As illustrated by Luke's story, if you retire in the year in which you are 55 or older, you can pull money out of your 401(k) as long as it's the 401(k) you had at your retiring employer and avoid the 10% penalty. If you roll this money into an IRA you lose this ability.

Looking at all your accounts and having a good understanding of what your income needs will be before 59 ½ will allow your financial planner to advise you on whether or not you should be rolling other 401(k) accounts into your retiring plan, and even IRA accounts. This should be done before you leave your employer.

Traditional, SIMPLE, and SEP IRA's

The rules for Traditional, SIMPLE and SEP IRA's is that you cannot take money before you are 59 ½ years of age or you will have a 10% tax penalty PLUS have 100% of the distribution added to you income for the year. So generally, taking money out of these plans will increase your tax bracket.

The rule to remember: If you leave your employer between the ages of 55 and 59 ½, you can pull income from the retirement account you had at the employer you last left. If this money is rolled to an IRA you can not take a distribution without a 10% penalty and taxes. Beware of an advisor that tries to get you to roll all of your money over without leaving a portion for emergencies and current income needs until 59 ½, unless you have substantial non-retirement assets.

Roth IRA's

Roth IRA's will have a 10% penalty plus taxes on any gains if you pull before 59 ½. You can pull your cost basis (or contribution amount) out without any tax consequences if you have had your account for at least 5 years.

If you are not 59 ½ and need income, you may want to consider utilizing your cost basis in your Roth IRA in order to reduce your tax burden.

Let's look at Suzie's situation:

> Suzie contributed $5,000 for 20 years at 8% earnings. Her value is $247,115. She has a cost basis of $100,000 ($5k x 20 years), and earnings of $147,115. Suzie can withdraw the full $100,000 without any tax implications, and she doesn't have to pay it back. If she touches the $147,115 before 59 ½ she will have a 10% penalty plus taxes. If she waits till she is 59 ½ or older, she can then take all the earnings tax free.

RMD's

Required Minimum Distributions, or RMD's, are the IRS's way of *making* you pay taxes. Some retirees won't notice them because they are already fulfilling their amounts because they rely on the income to survive and take a higher amount out than require.

Retirees, who aren't withdrawing anything or at least the minimums, get pretty annoyed with RMD's. All of a sudden, clients have to draw down their savings and pay taxes. It's not a fun situation.

Clients ask me all the time how much their RMD will be the following year. I can never tell them. The problem is that the IRS has a formula that takes the December 31st value on the previous year statement to calculate the amount.

The goal of the RMD is to run your account out by the time you die. That way, the IRS collects taxes from money that has never been collected on before.

A big problem is that the calculation expectations of your death can be sooner than your actual death. So the older you get, the higher the percentage of your account you have to pull.

The IRS doesn't care about which retirement account you pull from – only that you pull out a minimum amount each year to satisfy their tax collections. So if you have multiple accounts, or guaranteed streams of income on your IRA's, you can actually choose which accounts you pull from. This can be beneficial if you have accounts earning higher rates or guaranteed amounts of income investments in your IRA's that you aren't fully utilizing.

> **Hear It From An Expert:** If you do not fulfill your RMD, you will receive a 50% tax penalty on the amount not withdrawn plus ordinary income taxes. So not fulfilling your RMD is costly! While you can choose to reinvest your RMD in a non-retirement account if you do not need it, remember, if you reinvest it, you still have to pay taxes on it!

Myth #2: If a strategy exists, you should use it.

Retiring Early – Pro's, Con's and Should you Utilize 72T's?

For most retirement plans the IRS determined that 59 ½ is when you should be able to pull money from your retirement accounts and annuities. So how do you retire earlier if you haven't reached 59 ½ and most of your money is tied up in retirement and/or annuity accounts? How can you pull money out without getting hit with a 10% penalty? Read on…

72T's and IRA's – Pros and Cons

If you retire at age 50 or older, but you aren't 59 ½, you may want to consider a 72T Distribution. It's really important you fully understand the 72T. With this option, you will not have to pay the 10% penalty. However, you will have to take the exact same amount out for 5 years or until you are 59 ½, whichever is *greater*.

Let's look at an example.

- Craig retired when he was 52. He decided to take a 72T. He has to take the same amount every year until he is 59 ½. This means he has 7.5 years that he must take the same amount – not a penny more or a penny less.

- Stan retired at 57. He decided to take a 72T. He has to take the same amount every year until he is 62. This means he has five years that he must take the same amount – not a penny more or a penny less.

If either Craig or Stan stop taking the same distribution, they will be assessed a 10% penalty on all the money they have taken out over the years in which they started the 72T.

The pros of the 72T are simple:

- Avoiding the 10% penalty. This can obviously save quite a bit of money over the years.
- There is a one time exception that will allow you to recalculate your 72T.

The cons of the 72T are the following:

- Having the same amount of income each year – sometimes you may have a higher income need in the beginning but not for the entire time the 72T requires you to withdrawal money

- Not getting a high enough income – there is a formula that determines how much money you can receive on a 72T. The government doesn't want you to spend all of your money so they actually limit the amount you can take. The formula involves the treasury rate so the past few years really limited retirees on how much their distribution could be since rates were at all-time lows.

- Having an emergency need. If you have an emergency and need more money, you *cannot* pull more money out of the IRA account you are using for your 72T or you will owe the IRS 10% on all your previous distributions. It is really important that you work with a financial planner who understands how to maximize your 72T for your income needs, while moving your IRA money into another bucket just in case you do come across a situation where you need to pull more money out of your IRA. The splitting of your IRA into several buckets *before* you start your 72T could save you a lot of money in the future.

- Not needing the money but still having to take it out. In the recent years when our economy has been challenging, many people in their 50's experienced layoffs. Instead of looking at which accounts to pull from and how to strategically take distributions, they were ill advised to start 72T's on their IRA's. So they started the income stream, eventually got another job, and were stuck in the 72T or would owe back taxes. This meant that they had to continue to spend down their IRA's and pay a portion of it to the IRS when they didn't need it.

Myth#3: If your friend is doing something in retirement, then you should too

Dan and Amelia's Retirement Story:

Dan and Amelia came to see me because they were getting ready to retire. They had been saving their entire life, but, they were paying a lot in taxes and it really reduced what they were able to save. When they came to see me, Dan was only putting in 5% of his salary, which equated to $5,500, in his 401(k). When I asked him why he wasn't maxing out, he told me that he was.

"You can put $17,500 plus another $5,500 in for your catch up contribution. This means that you wouldn't have to pay taxes this year on $23,000."

"No, Rob told me I can only put in the match."

"Who's Rob?" I asked.

"My buddy at work. He's pretty financially savvy."

"Well, Rob's been costing you thousands of dollars a year in taxes because he isn't correct."

Amelia chimed in, "I told him that he needed to ask his HR department and not just believe Rob. I kept reading that he could add more!"

I still don't know if Dan has heard the end of it from Amelia…

Your friends at work are good people. But it pays to double check if what they say is correct when it has to do with your financial situation.

The Water cooler talk

We've all done it. We go to work and start talking about our lives. The conversation may involve a new diet, where to go on your next vacation, or finances.

A popular topic around the water cooler seems to revolve around company benefits. More often than not, employees listen to other employees about which benefits to choose and what the rules and laws are regarding their retirement plans.

I believe there are more mistakes made on 401(k)'s because of water cooler talk. Clients will come in and tell me what their buddy at work said and why they decided to not invest in their 401(k), how they decided to invest, or what amount they can contribute. 9 times out of 10 they have the wrong information.

> **Hear It From An Expert:** Water cooler talk usually involves stock tips, 401(k) advice, or other advice about benefits at work. Do your homework - remember, financial planning isn't one size fits all and what may be right for your co-workers isn't necessarily right for you and your family. Consult your financial planner who knows the intricate details of your financial plan before acting on co-workers financial advice.

Pensions

Myth #4: It's an easy choice whether to take a pension rollover or buyout.

In the last five years, the number of pension buyouts has drastically increased. This is where a retiree who is currently getting pension income is offered a lump sum amount from their former employer.

> Gary's Pension Story:
> Gary had received a pension buyout offer from Ford and called me to see what he should do.
>
> Although Gary had been retired for over 10 years, he was being offered a pension buyout on a survivor pension benefit he was receiving from his wife who had passed away 10 years prior.
>
> Gary and Cindy had both lost their spouses and were fortunate to find love again. They were avid bikers and met on a 100 mile cycling race. I met this wonderful couple about 5 years into their new marriage.

They are in their 60's and both had worked 30 years for their previous employers and were able to retire when they were only in their 50's.

When Gary first called me, he told me how they met and how he had been offered a buyout from Ford. Gary told me that they were offering $500,000. If Gary decided to take this buyout, then he would no longer receive the $35,000 of income per year that Ford was paying him.

"I'm guessing that I should not take this buyout because I would have to earn 7% in order to receive the same income," Gary said to me.

"Actually, for your situation it isn't that cut and dry," I told him. "I know from our previous conversations that you and Cindy want to make sure that in the event of either of your deaths that the other spouse is taken care of. Since this is your deceased spouse's pension benefit, the $35,000 stops if you die. Cindy gets no further income."

"Oh. I never thought about that," Gary said.

After talking extensively to Gary, I told him that we needed to run some pension calculations to see how Cindy would be affected if Gary died. We reviewed their goals, lifestyle and tax situation. We also talked about Gary's concern of Cindy being taken care of should something happen to him.

After looking at all the taxes that Gary and Cindy were paying on the current income stream, I pointed out that they were paying 35% Federal taxes and another 4.25% State taxes on the $35,000 of income Gary currently received from the pension benefit. After paying $13,737.50 in taxes, the remaining $21,262.50 of the pension income was going into their savings account each year. By rolling the lump sum into the IRA, Gary and Cindy could control when they pulled out for income until Gary was 70 ½ and had to start taking his Required Minimum Distributions (RMD's). In 10 years they would save over $130,000 in taxes just by keeping it in the IRA instead of it being distributed!

After talking about the pros and cons, we decided that we were going to roll the lump sum into an IRA Annuity that had a living benefit (guaranteed income stream for both Gary and Cindy's lifetime). We also decided that they would waited to pull it until 70 ½ when Gary had to take his RMD.

The story doesn't end here. A few months later I got a phone call from Cindy. "I just got a buyout package from FedEx. I'm assuming that we should accept it?" she asked.

"Not necessarily. We need to run some more pension calculations," I said.

FedEx was offering Cindy $750,000. Cindy was currently receiving $65,000 per year. Gary was the beneficiary and if something happened to Cindy he would continue to receive $65,000 for the remainder of his life. After running calculations it was clear that Cindy should turn it down. It just wasn't a high enough buyout amount to compensate for the $65,000 of lost income. Cindy and Gary relied on the $65,000 of income for their living expenses. Neither Cindy nor Gary had children and all their assets were going to charity upon their deaths. This time, it just didn't make sense for them to roll it over.

Cindy turned the pension offer down. Cindy is continuing to receive her $65,000 per year in income. She called me the other day to tell me she just booked a surprise trip for Gary and her to bike around France for their anniversary. I'm hoping to see pictures soon!

A pension is income a retiree receives from their previous employer for the remainder of their life. It is a set amount and may or may not have an income benefit for their spouse should they die first. While every pension differs, pensions will have a vesting period (i.e. 10 years) that an employee must work in order to qualify for an income benefit upon retirement. Pensions also differ as far as what age a retiree can draw the income out (60, 65, etc.) Pension income is taxed in the year in which it is received.

If you have a pension, then look at it closely. The amount that is being estimated is usually based on straight life. If you are married, then this means that upon your death all income stops. Your spouse will not receive any benefit from your pension upon your death.

The pension landscape had changed quite a bit in the last few years. Many employers are offering lump sum options, as well as lifetime incomes. It is imperative you find a financial planner who can run pension calculations for you before choosing which option to take.

Lifetime income streams normally give you the option to take a straight life – meaning that once you die it stops. This will have a higher benefit for your lifetime than if you take a spousal option.

Spousal options can range from your spouse continuing to receive 100%, 75%, 50%, or some other percentage of your income. This will lower your check compared to if you took straight life, but, it gives your spouse some protection.

Lump sum benefits allow you to roll your pension to an IRA in order to avoid taxes, potentially give you and your spouse the same income stream, and also give you the ability to pass on any remaining amounts to your beneficiaries.

There are many factors that we have to take into consideration when looking at which pension options to take. Lifetime expectancies, income needs, inflation, social security amounts, debts, existing assets, and lifestyles and goals should all be discussed and accounted for.

Having pension calculations run can give you the education and information you need to make the right decision for both yourself and your family. Let's take a look at what happened to Karl and Kasey.

Karl and Kasey's Pension Story:
Karl and Kasey came to my firm because they had received a pension buyout. Kasey had worked for 30 years at her employer and had left to start a new career. One day she opened her mail and although she is in her mid- 40's, the pension department at her old employer was requiring her to take a lump sum payout or start pension income now.

After creating a plan that was specific to Karl and Kasey's personal lifestyle, it was clear that although it was tempting to take the income now, if they did this they would never retire.

By taking the lump sum pension amount and rolling it to an IRA, we were able to grow the money, and give them a potential income that was two to three times the amount they were able to pull now. In addition, after factoring in the after tax amount of the pension that they could have received now and invested, it was also two to three times less than what they would have if we took the lump sum and earned the same rates.

By taking the lump sum and rolling their money to an IRA, it was also clear that Kasey had a much better chance of retiring at 60 vs. taking the income now and having to work into her 80's.

Hear It From An Expert: Making pension elections is a major decision. You owe it to yourself and your family to take the time and do your homework. Working with a competent financial planner who can show you different scenarios is essential to making an educated decision.

Chapter 7
FINANCIAL PLANNING EXPOSED:
EMOTIONAL BAGGAGE

Myth #1: What you buy today will be the same tomorrow.

Myth #2: If you are a conservative investor, then you should not take advantage of your employer's retirement plan.

Myth #3: Holding onto investments that you've always had, is a smart strategy.

Myth #4: Cash is king.

Myth #5: You owe it to your kids to pay for college.

"I walk down the street.
There is a deep hole in the sidewalk.
I fall in.
I am lost... I am helpless.
It isn't my fault.
It takes forever to find a way out.

I walk down the same street.
There is a deep hole in the sidewalk.
I pretend I don't see it.
I fall in again.
I can't believe I am in the same place.

But, it isn't my fault.
It still takes me a long time to get out.

I walk down the same street.
There is a deep hole in the sidewalk.
I see it is there.
I still fall in. It's a habit.
My eyes are open.
I know where I am.
It is my fault. I get out immediately.

I walk down the same street.
There is a deep hole in the sidewalk.
I walk around it.

I walk down another street."

— *Portia Nelson, There's a Hole in My Sidewalk: The Romance of Self-Discovery*

The stories I've heard in the Financial Planning world break my heart and reflect many qualities of the poem above. Some potential clients pretend not to see the hole, or the money issues in their life. Other potential clients clearly see the issues and ignore them. My clients and I talk regularly about the issues, (scary and otherwise) so I can get them on the right road- allowing them to miss the potholes of poor decisions or planning.

There are many types of emotional baggage, but no particular type is greater than the baggage that comes with guilt. From grandparents who want to provide for their grandchildren, to spouses that aren't communicating correctly about spending habits. Even if you've inherited your money, you still need to make good choices to keep that money. The people who have saved should not feel guilt for making good financial decisions. I tell my clients to remember, "Don't go to extremes." It's okay to save and spend- really!

Whether it be earned or inherited, women especially feel guilt around finances. Furthermore, I've especially noticed people who make poor decisions or live paycheck to paycheck seem to have a completely different view of money. Sometimes, there is a guilt that their actions have taken them to that place. Sometimes there isn't. However, the guilt of money has affected us all at one time or another. The guilt that we sometimes feel is often placed from our own mind by what our minds or others have told us, "We have to do."

Hear It From An Expert: Money doesn't just *happen* to people. Poor money choices are a cycle of bad behavior. You have the power to break the cycle and rise above. There is no time that is too late to make better financial choices.

Grace's Retirement Story:

Grace is one of my favorite clients. At 80 years old, she had gone through the Great Depression and understood difficult financial choices because she saw the direct repercussions. Grace had debilitating emotional baggage concerning her finances and spending money. She believed there was never going to be enough money in her investment accounts so she saved and penny-pinched to an extreme. Grace only lived off her social security, even though she had over a million dollars. Grace confided in me one day that she wished she could take her grandchildren to Disney, just once. I looked over her portfolio and arranged the trip, even putting Grace in touch with a vacation planner. She ended up taking her grandkids to Disney that same year. Having such an incredible time, Grace chose to do the trip again next year. I explained to her, "There needs to be a balance between living and saving. If you can afford it, memories are worth spending the extra money."

Hear It From An Expert: Knowing what to save and what to spend is crucial. Poor money choices are chosen. Whether consciously or subconsciously, we make choices every day. Please work with your financial planner to find a balance between saving and spending that works for you.

Myth #1: What you buy today will be the same tomorrow.

Jack's Retirement Story:

Jack was referred to me from another client. He came to see me because he didn't understand why his investments weren't increasing. He had the same advisor since the 90's, during which he had made substantial gains up until 2000. However, since then, he just couldn't' seem to get decent returns. He told me that once a year he met with his advisor and said that the last six years he had been asking why this was occurring and if they should go into a different investment, but his advisor told him each year that he shouldn't sell it when it was down and that he needed to keep his long term goals in mind.

I looked at Jack's statements and it didn't take long to figure out why he hadn't recouped much of his losses. Jack was in every stock that was hot in the 90's. In fact, 60% of his portfolio was constructed of the hot technology stocks of the 90's. Many of these stocks had fallen to penny stock status. The reality of Jack recouping any of his losses was going to be slim if Jack kept his current portfolio.

I explained to Jack that buy and hold only works if the companies you buy are still the same companies you originally bought. Many of these companies had gone through mergers and acquisitions and were no longer even in the same line of business. I also told him sometimes it's best to cut your losses in order for you to move forward.

We reconstructed Jack's portfolio and he's been making nice gains over the last few years. However, since Jack is retired and living off his investments, he probably will never see the account rebound to the level it once was.

If your advisor doesn't have discretion on your account, then they can't make changes without your permission. When clients first come to me, I hear over and over how their current advisor isn't contacting them. The bad news about not hearing from your advisor is if you haven't given them discretion, then they can't make changes. So as the market and economy change, your account won't.

If your advisor does have discretion, but you aren't hearing from them, then you take the risk that your goals and risk tolerance may have changed. Without a conversation, they are not legally allowed to change your account objective. So if you were an aggressive investor and now you are nearing retirement, they can't just change your objective to a moderate or conservative risk level without you agreeing to it. So, what was ok when you were in your early 50's may not be ok when you are nearing your 60's.

Investments change over time – a company's management and philosophy can change which means the stock you bought 10 years ago may have the same name but not be the same company. Mutual fund management teams change which directs the fund decisions. What was hot five years ago isn't hot today. Interest rates move which changes the direction of bond prices and the entire bond landscape.

The bottom line is this: the market and economic landscape changes constantly and the person directing your investment portfolio should be on top of what is going on. Just because an individual is licensed to sell investments doesn't mean they should. Financial advisors all have different philosophies. Talk to 10 different advisors and you will get five advisors who have no philosophy and five advisors who each have a different philosophy.

The person you choose to handle your investments should have a philosophy and process they can discuss with you. Ask your advisor how they keep up with the overall market and economic landscape and how they utilize that information to monitor your portfolio. If they can't articulate to you their process in a way that makes sense to you – run. If you never hear from your advisor – run. If you have the same investments year after year without any changes based on what's happening in the market and economy – run.

This is your money and your livelihood. Don't settle for mediocrity.

Myth #2: If you are a conservative investor, then you should not take advantage of your employer's retirement plan.

Hear It From An Expert: Many individuals still have a significant fear of the market. As long as your employer retirement plan is *not* a non-qualified deferred compensation plan (NQDC), then your employer does *not* have access to the money you contribute to your plan. If you have a 401(k), 403B, 457 or SIMPLE IRA account, the company cannot use your money and it is not an asset for creditors of the company to go after. If you *do* have a non-qualified deferred compensation plan (NQDC), then different rules exist and your contributions can be up for grabs by creditors of your company.

A Note on Indecision and Fear

There is fear on one side and greed on another. When looking at your investments you really want to be in the middle. The problem occurs when you get out of balance. This tends to happen based on how the market is performing.

When the market is rallying, people tend to get greedy. When the market is struggling, people tend to get fearful. The recent bear market of 2000 to 2012 really wreaked havoc on investors portfolio's and thus sent many investors all the way to the fear side.

This fear has really caused many people of working age to make bad decisions regarding their employer retirement plans. Many people have stopped contributing to their plans. They no longer get tax deductions because they aren't contributing, they aren't growing their savings, they haven't received employer match money, and they have missed out on buying while the market was low. People have basically allowed fear to rule their financial decisions and now they are even further off track.

Not contributing to your employer plan because you are fearful of the market is a big mistake. The Department of Labor has stipulated that many different asset classes are required to be in employer retirement plans. Whether you are the most conservative investor, or the most aggressive, if you have an employer plan that you are eligible to contribute your own money to, there should be some investment solution for you.

Zach's Retirement Story:

Zach had not invested in his employer's plan for over eight years when he came to see me- big mistake! He wasn't sure about the stock market, so Zach simply decided not to make any decision at all. He was looking to retire in the next 10 years, but he truly wasn't prepared. Zach had saved $550,000 in cash and was earning half a percentage of interest at his local credit union. He worked for a company that matched 5% of whatever he put into the plan. Zach's annual salary was $110,000 and his effective tax rate was 19%. For every $10,000 Zach put into his plan, he would have saved $1,900 in taxes. Over eight years that equated to a tax bill of $15,200!

In addition to the lost tax savings, Zach was losing out in an employer match of $5,500 per year. That equated to $44,000 over eight years. Keep in mind that this was *before* he even made a penny of interest!

When I showed Zach all that he had been missing out he told me that he had never really looked at it that way. I also showed him that his plan did offer conservative options if he really wanted to reduce his market risk.

Zach is now investing in his plan and taking full advantage of it. He is on track to retire and is looking at what state he wants to reside in upon retirement.

Hear It From An Expert: Don't let fear or greed drive your investment decisions. Remember, this is your financial future and the decisions you make today will have a dramatic effect on tomorrow.

Myth #3: Holding onto investments that you've always had, is a smart strategy.

Holding onto investments that you inherited or that you've owned your entire life because you're emotionally tied to them is not in your best interest. *There. I said it.*

If the investment you hold is no longer the same company it used to be, no longer pays good dividends, no longer is poised for growth, no longer meets your financial objectives – get rid of it!

Now, I realize some people have big holdings in non-retirement accounts and may need to sell over several years to reduce the taxable burden. But *stop* holding onto investments that aren't going to help you achieve your goals.

The world is constantly changing. Companies are constantly changing. Your goals will be met with the proper investments. If it doesn't work, dump it. *Move on.* Having greater than 5% of your total portfolio value in a specific investment can create an unnecessary risk in your financial future. Diversifying a portion of your holding will help reduce your overall risk.

Diversification is key. Living in Michigan, I have a lot of automotive clients. Many of my clients had General Motors stock they had held since the 1950's or inherited. Before the big bankruptcy of GM, I was telling clients to diversify. Although most took my advice, some clients were just too emotionally attached to their GM stock.

"My dad worked there his entire life."

"I inherited this from my family trust."

"GM is a solid company."

"GM's always been good to me."

Once the bankruptcy occurred, we heard new comments like, "When do I get the shares of the new stock?" Unfortunately, some clients hadn't been listening very closely.

When a stock goes bankrupt shareholders of common stock are last in line to receive anything. Owning stock is just that – ownership. You take the risk of losing it all if the company doesn't perform well.

For owners of GM common stock before the bankruptcy, the reality is they didn't get new stock. So the new stock you see doing well now, doesn't mean anything to the people who had held stock since 1950.

Burt and Anna's Retirement Story:

Burt had been buying stock since 1970 when he started working at GM. He retired in 2000 at age 60. Burt and Anna had a modest lifestyle and were enjoying retirement. They lived off Burt's pension, their social security and dividends from their GM stock and the Required Minimum Distributions (RMD's) that Burt had to take out of his retirement account.

His retirement account had GM in it and 80% of his non retirement assets were GM. For years I had been talking to him about diversifying. He just would not sell his GM.

Burt had over $750,000 tied up in GM stock in his retirement account and another $200,000 in non-retirement money. The GM bankruptcy took his $950,000 value down to pennies.

When the new GM stock came out I received a phone call from Burt. "When do I get my new stock?" he asked. I explained again to him how he was last in line and would not be getting any stock. It was a hard conversation. My heart when out to him and his wife.

Burt is 75 and is now living on his social security, GM pension, and the remaining $50,000 left in non GM investments. Anna, who is 67, will no longer receive pension income if Burt dies first because he choose straight life on his pension thinking that she could live off the GM stock if he died first.

Unfortunately, because of the GM concentrated holding that was in their investment portfolio, Anna will fall into poverty upon Burt's death. It's a horrible situation - especially because Burt and Anna did everything right with regards to their choices in saving. If only they had not let emotional attachment get in the way.

Hear It From An Expert: Have a plan with your financial planner on how to diversify your concentrated investment holdings. Take emotions out of your decisions.

Myth #4: Cash is king

When I started my career, I could get my clients an 8% rate for their money markets. They had access to it on any day. There was no timeframe that they had to be in the money market. It was a great place for emergency money.

The Federal Reserve had interest rates at or near zero for five years. *5 years!* This meant that investors who kept their money in cash at the bank earned next to nothing if anything at all!

You need your money working hard for you. Keeping excess cash earning low interest rates may actually look like you're doing well, but in reality you are losing money because the cost of living is always going up.

You need three to six months of living expenses in the bank in case you have an emergency. Unless you have a big project in the near future, any excess amount sitting in cash earning nothing is harming you.

The reason it's hurting you is because the $1 you spend today, won't get you the same thing in a year or two. We can't stop time and inflation, so we need to make sure that our money is working hard for us and at the very least keeping up with inflation.

Mary's Retirement Story:

Mary was 53, wanted to retire at 60, and had $300,000 in the bank. Her emergency savings of six months would require her to only keep $24,000 in the bank. Mary didn't know what to do with the excess cash she had because she didn't understand investing and didn't think she had enough money to go see a financial planner. She had inherited a part of her account and had also been adding $1,500 each month to her savings account. Mary thought that she was on track to meet her retirement goal because she had saved so much.

Mary came to see me because her friend had referred her to me. She didn't know what the big deal was but her friend kept telling her that she had too much cash in the bank. Her friend understood inflation and making your money work for you. Mary wasn't quite there yet.

When we discussed Mary's goals, Mary told me that she was earning money because her statement always went up. I showed Mary the big 0% that was listed on her rate of return. I also showed her how her statement was always up because her "earnings" equaled what was being contributed. I then ran figures to show her the difference of earning 0% verse if she had been earning 6%.

Mary was flabbergasted when I showed her that if she had earned 6% on her money that she would have an extra $75,200!

I created a full financial plan for Mary, started investing her excess cash, and continued to educate Mary about interest, inflation and how her money could work for her.

Mary just retired at 61. She has been a great client and really learned a great deal about her financial situation. I'm really proud of her!

Hear It From An Expert: You work hard for your money so make it work hard for you! Making sure that you have a cash surplus plan can be critical to your retirement success!

Myth #5: You owe it to your kids to pay for college.

College is one of the hardest subjects when meeting with my clients. In many cases, paying for the children's college fund absolutely depletes the retirement account. So many people sign up for loans without consulting their financial planner.

As someone who paid for their own education, I understand not wanting your children to graduate with debt. However, before you retire, make sure that you take a realistic look at whether or not this is going to impact your retirement.

With the constant increase in tuition, room, board and books, it's not a big surprise most American's are unprepared for the cost of college. Even those parents who have college funds for their children often fall short. They started too late, didn't contribute enough, or lost money in the recent stock market decline in the 2000's.

I often have individuals come to me when their children are about to start college. They typically are in their late 40's to early 50's and want to retire in the next 10 to 20 years. Their children will soon be starting college and they want to know the best way to fund it.

In my experience, one of the first places people look to pay for their children's college is their IRA's or employer plans. Parents typically aren't thinking about how distributions from an IRA or loans on their employer plan will affect them in the long term. The desire to help their child get the best start in their adult life is the only thing they are thinking of. As a mom, I get it. As a financial planner, it's my job to help my clients take a realistic look at how this will affect them in the long term and to come up with a solution that financially makes the most sense.

Let's first talk about IRA's. There is a misconception you can take a loan from your IRA. IRA's do not permit for loans. You have the choice to either take a distribution or pay the taxes and possible penalties.

Parents are often shocked when I tell them what their distribution will cost them in taxes. The shock sets in even further when I show them how it will affect their retirement as well.

You also may be able to take your IRA money and roll it into your current employer's retirement plan that may allow for loans. Taking a loan from your employer's plan has consequences that you should be aware of.

If you take a loan from your employer's plan, how much you can take will be capped. You also will have to pay the loan back while you are working. You will not pay taxes on this money if you pay it back in full. If you leave your job and have not paid it back in full, you will have a 10% penalty if you are under 59 ½, plus everything will get added to your income for the year and you will pay ordinary income tax as well.

When you take a loan from your employer's retirement plan, not only do you pay interest, but you are creating a double tax situation. Money you receive in the loan amount has never been taxed. When you pay the loan back, your payments are no longer non-taxable payments – they are actually after tax payments. So even though it comes through your paycheck, you are taxed on the repayments in the current calendar year. This money then goes into your plan to pay interest and the loan amount back. Eventually, when you retire and take distributions from your plan, you are taxed again on this money.

Another negative to taking a loan from your employer's retirement plan is that often you are not able to afford to keep contributing towards your retirement. This may contribute to you not meeting your retirement goal. This could cause you to work longer, drastically reduce your standard of living, or not be able to retire at all.

Due to the complication and high cost associated with college, I've had clients who wanted to pay for their children's college but had to decide their child would have to get loans. I also have clients who decided to pay for a portion verse the entire cost and supplement the rest with loans.

Parents need to be more realistic. Children can go to community college for two years to save money. As a parent, you have the opportunity to teach great money choices that will affect their future. Teaching your children about the importance of smart financial choices starts with you. Parents shouldn't have debt for college, without first understanding how the debt impacts their own future.

Sometimes clients come to me and they have taken out large loans in their name. They want to retire but aren't sure how they are going to pay the loans off. I've seen loans in the amount of $100,000 plus and it often seems to sneak up on parents. The years go by quickly and all of a sudden high loans are established.

Nicole and Carl's Retirement Story:
Nicole and Carl have two children. They are paying for their college and took money out in the form of loans in their name. Both their children had money in accounts that Nicole and Carl had saved for them but Nicole didn't want to utilize it because she wanted their children to have money for their post college future.

Although Nicole and Carl have saved well and established a nice nest egg, they hadn't created a plan when they started taking out loans regarding the repayment. They were thinking of taking out a loan against their retirement plan through their employers but they weren't sure how it worked or if that was the best option.

I ran several different scenarios for Nicole and Carl. We discussed using the children's accounts since this was for their education. We also talked about the ramifications of retirement plan loans versus taking out a lump sum and just paying the taxes. We considered using their current income to make payments both on loans and also on tuition payments going forward.

After looking at all the options, we ultimately decided to utilize several different strategies for them including cashing out the children's accounts and reducing their luxury expenses in order to make monthly payments and get the loans paid off before retirement.

We also had to address the fact that their daughter had two more years until graduation and their son had one remaining year. We came up with a strategy and Nicole and Carl also decided the post graduate school that their daughter would need to attend would have to be a cost that she paid for herself.

Nicole and Carl are well on their way to a financially strong retirement and they should be free of all college debt in the next two years before they retire. Their children will both graduate with a Bachelor's Degree debt free as well.

However, I've had other clients who just aren't able to do this and they've had to make different decisions. Most importantly, we were strategic and creative to find an individual solution that would work for their family, but that's not always the first solution that's wanted. Working with your financial planner to find the best solution for your family- that's what matters!

Easton and Hannah's Retirement Story:

Easton and Hannah came to me because their son was about to graduate. They didn't have any money set aside for college and were at odds with each other about whether they should pay for his college or not.

Easton was firm that they were going to pay for his college and Hannah thought that their son should get loans. They only had a portion of their retirement saved and wanted to retire in the next 15 years. If they were going to meet their goal, they were going to have to really start putting money aside for retirement.

I ran a financial plan showing Easton and Hannah how utilizing their income now for college would make it so they had to work until 84. I also ran a scenario showing them if they put their income aside for retirement how they could retire at 68.

Looking at their full situation and the effects that paying for college would have on their retirement solved the fight. Easton took a look at me and said, "Ok, he can get loans."

I've also had clients who were able to reduce their current expenses and pay for college out of their current income.

Jerome and Paula's Retirement Story:

When Jerome and Paula first came to me, they were just about to start paying for the first of five children to go to college with all five children at some point, being in college at the same time. It was an overwhelming situation. We took a strategic look into all their financial information and discussed how Jerome and Paula could reduce their expenses. Additionally, we looked into having college paid for with their current income and bonus money that Jerome received each year.

We found that if they followed the plan and then redirected that money towards their retirement after the college bills were gone, they would still be on track for retirement.

Jerome and Paula really learned how to balance their cash flow and make sure they were putting money aside each month so when the tuition bill came they had the money to pay it. All five children now have their degrees and Jerome and Paula are now putting extra money towards their retirement.

Hear It From An Expert: Students can get loans for college. Retirees cannot get loans for retirement.

Chapter 8
FINANCIAL PLANNING EXPOSED:
CRUCIAL CONVERSATIONS WITH FAMILY

Myth #1: Your spouse, partner, or child doesn't need to be a part of financial planning.

Myth #2: Women don't have unique financial risks and needs- it's all just a bunch of hype.

Myth #3: Talking about finances with your children isn't necessary until you get older and need help.

Myth #1: Your spouse, partner, or child doesn't need to be a part of financial planning.

"Divorce rates among couples over 50 have doubled in the last 20 years, according to a study by Bowling Green State University. In 1990, fewer than one in 10 people who divorced were 50 or older. In 2009, that figure was one in four."

(http://www.cnn.com/2012/06/24/living/baby-boomer-divorce/)

Out of all the money conversations we have, the most important conversation involves your planner and your family.

Your Financial Planner owes it to you to discuss these five key ideas and you owe it to your family to include them in the discussion.

It isn't as hard to run out of your money as you may think.
Taxes, increasing expenses, surprise medical bills, your child asking for help,

etc. are all examples of how your retirement can quickly get off track. Retiring too early, retiring with large amounts of debt, and retiring with unrealistic expectations of what amount of money you can pull from your savings are all common problems that can be prevented. We all have choices to make and it's up to you whether you decide to make your finances a priority. I've had a lot of people tell me that they regret *not* planning, but I've never had anyone tell me that they regret actually doing planning.

Taxes can really accelerate the rate at which your money declines.
I cannot stress this enough! Do *not* forget that you still have to pay taxes in retirement! This can significantly increase the amount of money you have to pull off your savings. Not preparing for your tax bill can be the main cause of running out of your money.

Your financial decisions impact others around you, especially your spouse and children.
When you have to make a pension or social security election or when you make a decision on a major purchase; these are just a few things that can seem small, but can *drastically* impact those around you. Retirement is supposed to be fun - the golden years! It isn't that you can't have a great life, but knowing what the consequences could be for choices you make before you make those choices could be one of the greatest gifts you ever give your family.

Unexpected things will happen in retirement, whether it's a declining housing market, a volatile stock market, or medical costs. Being able to fund unexpected expenses, as well as rebound from the unexpected is important and vital to your financial success.
If you decide to retire and you don't have adequate savings, and you are just able to pay your monthly living expenses, then you probably shouldn't be retiring. This is a huge reason I see retirees outliving their money. Having a nest egg to cover unexpected expenses is important. It's important to discuss with your financial planner about what you would do if unexpected expenses arise.

Good people make bad decisions and that can very easily change how you envisioned your life.
You'll read about Joe's story below. Joe was a really nice guy who made poor decisions that changed his retirement dreams and the life of his daughter. He had regret upon his death because of those decisions. Seeking out a financial planner to talk about possible risks to choices you are going to make before you make those choices is important. Fully understanding

those risks and listening to your planner is just as important.

Joe's Retirement Story:

Joe once told me that his financial decisions didn't have anything to do with his children. He was planning on spending every penny before he died and had no desire to leave anything behind. When I asked him what date he planned on dying, he laughed at my question.

Joe's income needs were only $40,000 per year after taxes. His social security and retirement savings should have been enough, but he decided that he was going to take his retirement account and pay the taxes and penalties in order to buy a vacation home. When I explained to him that he would run out of his money within five years if he did this he still told me he was going to buy the vacation home. "I've worked my entire life and I'm going to spend my money." Joe was adamant that he knew how long his money would last.

Did you notice how I said, "potential client?" Although Joe wanted me to manage his retirement account, I declined taking him on as a client since I knew that he was not going to take my advice, therefore, I couldn't add any value to his situation.

I actually ran into Joe in the grocery store three years after he retired. We were in the checkout lane and he asked me if he could come see me the next day. I gave him a time and wondered what our meeting would be about.

Joe came into my office and showed me his statements. Not only had he taken out the money he told me he was going to use for his vacation home, but he had taken an extra $75,000 out for a boat. Joe was now down to only $26,000 and based on the increased expenses he had for his vacation home and boat, he was scheduled to run out of his money within the next eight months. Joe looked at me and said, "I should have listened to you. My daughter told me that I can come live with her but I don't want to. What should I do?"

I asked Joe about his primary and vacation home's value. Joe explained that it was down 45% because of the recession. We went through all of Joe's expenses and determined that he would have to sell both his primary and vacation homes in order to generate enough money to create an income. He also would have to sell his boat at a loss. Joe then told me that he had also been diagnosed with Parkinson's disease and that the medicine wasn't covered by his insurance. He was paying over $300 per month for his new medications.

After reducing Joe's expenses down to the bare bones, it was determined that the best scenario was for Joe to move in with his daughter. Reality had finally set in and Joe knew he needed the cash he was generating from selling his remaining assets for his future medical care.

Joe's mistakes cost him his independence as well as his daughter's. While she never complained to me, whenever I would see Joe around town there was sadness in his eyes. He would tell me how wonderful his daughter was to take him in and how she took really great care of him. But he also made a point to tell me one day that his Parkinson's was getting worse and that he wasn't sure how much longer he was going to be able to drive his car. He also told me his daughter turned down a promotion at work because it involved travel and she didn't have the money to hire someone to come in and take care of Joe while she would have been traveling. Joe said that it would have cost $1,500 a month to have some in home help. "I would have been able to afford that had I listened to you when I retired."

Joe's story haunts me to this day, because it was completely preventable. He lost over $150,000 to the IRS when he took the large lump sums out of his retirement plan. He lost over $200,000 on his vacation home and over $50,000 on his primary residence. He also ended up selling his boat for a $33,000 loss.

Some of the biggest ways I've seen family members impacted by a retiree's decisions:

Unhappy Retirements

I often find that most people haven't really thought or discussed with their spouse/partner what they envision for their retirement. This can create a problem, a big problem. If you don't have a vision of what you want your retirement to look like then start dreaming! Talk with your spouse/partner and find out what they are envisioning. Dream big and then go talk with a financial planner to see if your dreams can become reality before you retire. Retiring without an idea of what you want it to look like can lead to depression, alcohol and drug abuse, health issues, divorce, and more unpleasant experiences. It can also make the life of your spouse or children miserable.

Medical Situations

Who in the family is in charge if you are unable to make decisions on your own behalf, what legal paperwork is in place to back that person's authority up, and what conversations have taken place so your advocate knows what should be done in certain situations. Not having a conversation with all your children about what should happen if certain medical conditions exist can really put a strain on the family dynamics. Children that have to make decisions on your health care may be doing so under your wishes, but unless you have clearly communicated to the family what your wishes are, siblings relationships can be strained.

Children's Relationships

I've actually witnessed sibling relationships be completely broken because of retirees making bad decisions which left them in financial ruin. One or several children step in and financially or physically help out and the other siblings don't. The other siblings may not be financially or physically able to do so and this can create animosity. Some siblings may just choose not to get involved. This can create ill feelings and destroy your children's relationships.

Repayment of Debt

I work with a lot of widows. I have consulted widows who were left nothing but debt, debt that they didn't know about. Debt that caused them to lose their homes and cars, debt that literally changed their lifestyle forever. I've also consulted with children who had a parent die only to have to repay their debt. Co-signing on houses, automobiles, credit cards, and other loans should be done very cautiously. If you are going to have a cosigner, having a life insurance policy to take care of the debt burden should something happen is a good way to protect your family.

Eric and Fran's Retirement Story:
Eric and Fran were married for 40 years. I met with both Fran and Eric because they were getting divorced, but looking for an amicable split. They wanted me to go through all their assets and come up with an equitable split.

As you can imagine, it wasn't a rosy pictured appointment. I started discussing their background information in order to get a picture of their assets and lifestyle. I could tell that Fran was pretty angry and when I started asking Eric when he had retired she interrupted.

"That's why we are getting a divorce. *He* decided to retire, didn't tell me, and met with his buddy who's *his* financial advisor. He said it was ok to retire, but didn't tell him that we wouldn't have any money to go on vacation, donate to our church, or even take our grandkids out to dinner. He went to *his* advisor and didn't even consult me." Eric just sat there looking sad. Fran went on.

"We had talked about Eric retiring at 65- not 60. I should have been consulted and warned that our lifestyle would completely change before he made this decision. I've asked to be a part of the financial meetings for years, but Eric always meets with *his* buddy on the golf course, at the country club, etc. I've never been invited or consulted and now look at what's happened to our life."

Eric started to apologize but Fran wasn't having it. We had to meet a few times in order to work everything out, but Eric and Fran did divorce. Their lifestyle was drastically cut down. Eric is still single but Fran ended up getting remarried a few years later. She came in to meet with me with her new husband and they constructed a plan together.

While Eric and Fran's story is sad, not everyone will end up divorced. But that doesn't mean they will be happy. One of the biggest gifts you can give yourself and your family is an honest financial checkup *before* you tell your employer that you are retiring. Turning in your retirement papers without doing your homework is not only a risk for you, but a huge risk for your spouse/partner and any children you may have. Not involving your spouse/partner in your decision to retire, or in the financial planning aspect is a huge risk to your family, as it directly affects them.

Myth #2: Women don't have unique financial risks and needs- it's all just a bunch of hype.

Anyone who knows me can attest that I am very passionate about educating women on finances. Although I truly feel women are becoming more independent and really starting to try and become educated on finances, there is still a huge disconnect for many women when it comes to finances.

I hear more women tell me that it's ok for them to *no*t be involved in their finances because, "my husband takes care of it all." I can assure you, this is *no*t ok.

According to the Allianz Women, Money & Power Study, females have a 90% chance that at some point in their life they will have to manage their finances all on their own. This means that as women, we simply cannot allow ourselves to stand on the sidelines unengaged. Furthermore, if you have a wife, you should be encouraging her to get engaged and stay engaged in the conversation.

Women need to feel more comfortable talking to friends about money.

Every woman needs a good financial planner who they can feel comfortable asking questions and getting further educated by.

One of the biggest comments I hear from women is that their current advisor (or their husband's advisor) speaks in a condescending way towards them and they feel intimidated. It's no wonder that 70% of all women fire their financial advisor within a year of becoming widowed!

I find that there is also a trend among women to feel they are not worth being protected.

Scott and Christine's Retirement Story:

Just the other day I had a conversation with my clients Scott and Christine.

We were discussing Scott's lack of life insurance. Christine told me "If something happens I can get scrimpy if I need to. There is no point increasing our expenses."

"For the $600 a year it will cost to get the insurance coverage you need, it's not worth you living in poverty the rest of your life." I adamantly told her. I told my client that, "every time I talk or met with Scott, he says, 'Just make sure my wife is taken care of.' You living in poverty should he die is not what he has in mind about making sure you are taken care of."

Scott looked at her and said, "This isn't even up for conversation. I'm applying for coverage. We won't even feel the payment."

Scott applied for coverage and we are in the process of getting his approval from the insurance company.

According to the Administration on Aging, over 80% of women who are now in poverty weren't when their husbands were alive. Proper financial planning could have prevented a lot of these tragedies. As women, we need to wake up and start taking control of our financial future. It's just too important to leave in someone else's hands who may, or may not be with us till the end.

Nancy's Retirement Story:

I met Nancy six months after her husband died. She woke up one day and could smell bacon cooking. She got dressed, came downstairs, and found her husband lying face down on the counter. Nick had a heart attack and died instantly. He was 58.

Nancy was two years older than Nick and had the ability to pull a widow's benefit from Social Security. It was a good thing because Nick had always taken care of the bills. He had let his life insurance lapse and Nancy was only left with a 401(k) account worth $250,000 and an IRA their financial advisor managed worth $45,000.

Nancy was a stay at home mom since she had her first baby at age 25. She had worked part time here and there, but always made under $10,000 per year. They had been living on a $100,000 plus income and had a nice lifestyle when Nick was alive.

Nancy knew that she had to change some things. She had gone to her financial advisor and didn't like how she was treated. She said that anytime she asked a question he kept patting her hand and saying, "Don't worry honey, I'll take care of you." All the while, her advisor was trying to get Nancy to roll her 401k over to his office.

Nancy didn't want to be taken care of. She wanted to know the full ramifications of her current financial situation and put a plan in place that moved her forward.

We went through all the changes Nancy was going to have to make. To be honest, it was overwhelming for me as well. Nancy had to change her lifestyle 180 degrees. Her income had been cut in half and there weren't adequate savings to support her for the next 20-40 years.

Nancy expressed to me how intimidating finances were to her. She told me that she had always been ok with Nick taking care of everything. We've had a lot of education meetings and although Nancy was intimidated at first, I think she's now a lot more comfortable with discussing and managing her finances than at first.

The most tragic part about Nancy's situation is it could have all been prevented. If annual reviews had been conducted with both Nancy and Nick, insurance would have been discussed and coverage probably wouldn't have lapsed. Nancy also would have been better prepared to handle the finances and not had to deal with the stress of money at a time when she was grieving the loss of her husband.

Nancy has adjusted to her lifestyle and has done excellent living within the budget we set for her. She doesn't get to do the things she envisioned in retirement, but she has a new-found empowerment in knowing she's educated about her finances, and her future.

Women need to be engaged in the financial conversation. As a husband, boyfriend, or even father, encourage the women in your life to be involved in financial conversations. No one knows what is going to happen when, but staying engaged in your financial plan is one of the best ways to start reversing the trend of women falling into poverty.

Hear It From An Expert: Women need to stop thinking its ok to sell themselves short. Women are falling into poverty at alarming rates. It's important for women to get involved and stay involved in their financial planning; the poverty epidemic is preventable.

Myth #3: Talking about finances with your children isn't necessary until you get older and need help.

With our life expectancy on the rise, chances are your children will at some point have to help take care of you and/or your spouse. While it may not mean you living with them, it probably involves someone stepping in to handle your finances.

However, having conversations with your children before this happens is important. The last thing you want to do is leave your children an unorganized mess so they are scrambling to be able to take care of you.

You should have important documents in order. Your Durable Power of Attorney will legally dictate who should handle your finances and make decisions on your behalf should you need someone to step in.

Make sure you choose a child who is financially responsible and competent. If you do not have a child meeting these requirements, then do *not* give them the power to handle your affairs.

Think about this for a moment. If your children can't handle their own finances, then how can they handle yours? If your children abuse debt, can't save, and/or don't have a financial plan for themselves, then how are they supposed to manage your life savings? If you do not have a financially responsible child, then look elsewhere. Find another relative, friend, or get a corporate trustee to handle your affairs should you become incompetent.

Meg and Charlie's Retirement Story:
Meg was a client of mine. She was 72 and had been saving her money all throughout her lifetime. She had built a substantial nest egg for herself and was financially independent.

I hadn't seen Meg for a while and had been calling but getting no response. I received a call one day from her son, Charlie. "My mom has dementia and I had to take over her finances. She never talked to me about this. I actually had no idea that I was going to be in charge of her finances should something happen. Can we meet so I can try and figure out what is going on?" Charlie asked me.

Charlie and I met and went through everything. He had no idea what his mother had saved. He was definitely shocked. I asked Charlie if he knew which bills needed to be paid, but he had no idea.

"My mom didn't tell me where her safety deposit key was. I can't find it and I know she left me instructions in there according to the attorney. The problem is, I can't get in the box. My mom shredded all of her documents religiously. Until stuff starts to come in, I just have no idea."

I gave Charlie the spreadsheet I had on his mom's expenses from our financial planning sheet. The good news was that she had no debt and very few bills.

"I just don't even know where to start. I don't know much about investments. Do I have to tell you what to pull off for her nursing home expenses, or do you decide where to get it?"

"I can advise you on that. Why don't I explain what I do and how I can fully help you?" I asked Charlie.

So we had an hour conversation on what my role was, what his new role was, and how I could best help him with his new duty.

Charlie ended up doing a great job for his mom. But, it was a confusing process. He never found the key to the safety deposit box and he had to wait until his mom's death in order to get into it. In it, was enough cash saved to pay for her nursing home, along with jewelry, and a written plan of what accounts to pull from.

Thankfully, Charlie and I worked together and managed to pay for his mom's expenses without depleting her accounts. But, what if we hadn't been able to do that? Because Meg never discussed with Charlie what he should do and where the key to her safety deposit box was. If her accounts had been depleted she would have had to qualify for Medicaid and wait to be admitted to a Medicaid nursing home; the standard of care would not have been the same.

Charlie and his two siblings all inherited a good amount of money. They are all clients of mine and we have talked with their adult children about what should happen if one of them is not able to handle the finances while they are alive. As Charlie said, "I don't want my children to deal with my finances unprepared."

A note on raising financially-fit children

With the possibility of your children someday having to step in and take care of your finances, raising responsible, financially fit children is important.

I truly believe that the sooner you start talking with your children about finance, the easier it will be for them to be financially literate. I grew up in a household where business was discussed, but finances weren't. I really believe if I had been given a stronger financial upbringing I would have made better decisions when I was younger.

I want my child to be financially literate. So when I had my son, Keegan, I thought about how I was going to have financial conversations with someone still little. I wondered at what age I was going to dispense advice. What I decided to do makes my husband laugh at me every month. However, this is how I'm teaching Keegan about money.

Keegan's Financial Literacy Story:
When my son was born, I started a college fund for him, immediately. Every month, I put money in and every month, I received a statement showing what I've contributed, what investment it went in, and any earning/losses.

I have all my statements on my investment accounts delivered to me online, except for Keegan's college account. I intentionally didn't switch it to online delivery because every month it comes, the magic happens. Keegan sits on my lap and I show him the college statement. I go through all the activity and talk to him about how he's going to have money to utilize for college.

My husband laughs at me, but I've done this since Keegan was one month old. I want my son to be comfortable reading statements, with the ups and downs of the market, and understand savings. I don't want him to be intimidated by or be uncomfortable around finances, and this is the only way I can think to educate him.

A note about teaching children to save

Another way to educate your children is to teach them to be great savers. You can either do this with an allowance they earn, or if they are older and receive any sort of wages. A great way to do this is by having them save half in a piggy bank or bank account and allowing them to spend the other half.

Hear It From An Expert: The more you discuss financial matters, the more comfortable you will become. If you are putting your children in charge of your affairs whether it's during your life, or upon your death, a conversation is warranted. Your financial planner should be able to facilitate a discussion between you and your children if needed. Introducing your children to your financial planner is a good idea so they can establish a relationship should they need to take charge of your finances. It's also a good idea to consider putting a clause into your estate planning document stating your children can receive 10% of their inheritance for each of the first 2 years, and then the rest in year 3. This gives your children time to work with a financial planner to avoid the pitfalls that can happen to individuals falling into great sums of wealth quickly.

In Conclusion

After being a financial advisor for over 5 years, I had one client story affect me on a deeper level than most. When a client's husband passed away, I realized during our emotional meeting that I didn't have the information to help her survive financially, after his death. At that moment, I realized I wasn't adding the value I truly wanted to add to my clients' lives. Shard Financial was born out of the desire to truly educate, prepare, and enlighten my clients during every step of their planning.

I hope after reading this you have a clearer understanding of why financial planning is so important to your financial success. While your investments are important, the other aspects of your finances are just as crucial. As many myths circulate the financial world, being able to talk with your financial planner about what is, and what isn't true, can help you avoid big pitfalls so you can ultimately achieve your own financial success.

As Yogi Berra best said, "If you don't know where you are going, you'll end up someplace else." A financial plan helps you get to where you are going. Not having a plan may just lead you somewhere you don't want to go.

Remember: It's your money, your life, and your future. Take the time to plan and work with a professional who can lead you in your journey, assist you in your stumbling along the way, and be the voice of clarity when you need it.

I think of my previous client every day and wish I held then the knowledge I hold now.

I believe passionately in the power of understanding financial planning and I'm honored to speak nationally and connect with clients on a personal level. I'd love to talk to you, please reach out if you have questions or I can be of any assistance.

ABOUT THE AUTHOR

Margie Shard, CFP ®, is a CERTIFIED FINANCIAL PLANNER™ and founder of Shard Financial Services, a planning and investment strategies firm in Fenton, MI. Margie's desire to stop the misinformation in the financial advisor industry stems from the disastrous situations she has witnessed since entering the industry in 2001.

Margie believes in keeping up on market and economic issues in order to help navigate her clients through the risks she sees developing in the markets. She is often found educating the public through her *"A Women's Conversation on Money"* discussion workshops, and bi-annual Market and Economic updates. Her radio show, *"The Margie Shard Show"*, also streams nationally via podcast.

Margie's entrepreneurial spirit has led her to create community events such as the *Shard Financial Back Pack Night (formerly Women, Wine, Fashion & Finance) Fundraiser* for the Food Bank of Eastern Michigan, as well as *100 Women Igniting Change*. She has received numerous accolades for both her professional and community work.

Find out more about Margie and follow her blog and radio show/podcast at: www.shardfinancial.com.

Made in the USA
Charleston, SC
20 January 2015